Stories of Serenity

52 Buddhist Tales to Transform Your Life

Ananda Ray

Foreword

Dear Reader,

Welcome to a contemplative exploration of life's essence through "Stories of Serenity: 52 Buddhist Tales to Transform Your Life." This collection presents a tapestry of Buddhist stories, curated to offer guidance and inspiration for navigating the complexities of modern life.

Throughout this book, you will encounter stories that resonate with universal themes such as gratitude, mindfulness, compassion, and resilience. Drawing from the rich tradition of Buddhist philosophy, each tale is carefully crafted to illuminate a specific aspect of human experience and offer practical insights for living a more meaningful and fulfilling life.

Structured to accompany you throughout the year, each of the 52 tales offers weekly guidance on the path to spiritual and personal growth. They unfold the virtues of empathy and awareness, encourage surrender to the flow of life, and remind us of the beauty in each moment's potential for transformation.

Imagine each story as a pebble cast into the still waters of your mind, where the ripples touch the shores of your consciousness in various forms. Some waves bring immediate clarity, while others gently reveal their depth over time. Every reflection, whether vivid or subtle, is a part of a bigger truth that connects us all.

Through these tales, we invite you to engage in life's puzzles and pleasures with a rejuvenated perspective.

As you turn these pages, some stories may bring a smile, others may provoke thought, or inspire a new way of seeing the world. Each narrative is an invitation to approach life with an open heart and an eager mind, cherishing and learning from each moment's uniqueness.

"Stories of Serenity" is more than just a book; it is a conduit between the enduring wisdom of Buddhism and the everyday challenges of modern life. It extends an invitation to weave these teachings into your personal narrative, encouraging you to uncover and foster your innate capacities for love, kindness, and understanding.

Whether you are new to Buddhism or have been on a spiritual path for many years, we believe that the wisdom contained within these pages has the power to transform your perspective and enrich your journey.

May these stories illuminate your path, reveal the treasures within your own spirit, and lay the groundwork for your ongoing growth and enlightenment. Let them show you that the truth you seek is already within you, waiting to be discovered and embraced.

With warmth and wisdom,

Ananda Ray

Table of Contents

Foreword... 2

1. The Mustard Seed. *The potential for immense growth within the tiniest of beginnings.*.. 9

2. The Blind Men and the Elephant. *The subjective nature of perception and the importance of holistic understanding.*......... 13

3. The Two Monks and the Woman. *The consequences of judgment and liberation found in forgiveness.*............................... 17

4. The Tiger and the Strawberry. *The power of presence and finding joy in the simplicity of life.*.. 19

5. The Stonecutter. *The journey of self-discovery and the realization of inner strength.*.. 23

6. The Four Wives. *The multifaceted nature of love and the depth of human relationships.*... 27

7. The Lost Sutra Scroll. *The enduring presence of wisdom, waiting to be unveiled.*.. 31

8. The Elephant Rope. *The breaking free from self-imposed limitations and realizing true potential.*............................ 35

9. The Dog's Empty Dream. *The nature of material pursuits and the search for true fulfillment.*.. 38

10. The Three Questions. *The pursuit of wisdom and self-discovery through introspection.*... 41

11. The Golden Fish. *The fleeting nature of desire and the true riches found within.*.. 45

12. The Salt Doll. *The dissolution of ego and the realization of oneness with the universe.*... 49

13. The Arrow Maker. *The importance of purpose and direction in the journey of life.*... 52

14. The Jar of Honey. *The sweetness of life's blessings and the appreciation of simple pleasures* 55

15. The Wise Parrot. *The wisdom found in unexpected places and the power of keen observation*.............................. 57

16. The Woodcutter's Wealth. *The rewards of hard work and the abundance found in gratitude*............................. 62

17. The Lotus Flower. *Purity and enlightenment, rising above adversity to bloom in beauty*............................. 65

18. The Precious Gem. *The value of inner richness over external wealth* 69

19. The Two Acrobats. *The balance between risk and trust in the pursuit of harmony*............................. 73

20. The Peacock's Dance. *The celebration of life and the expression of one's unique beauty*............................. 77

21. The Tree of Life. *The interconnectedness of all living beings and nurturing essence of nature*............................. 79

22. The Two Frogs. *The importance of courage and perseverance in the face of adversity*............................. 83

23. The Jewel in the Robe. *The hidden wisdom within simplicity and the discovery of inner riches*............................. 87

24. The Empty Boat. *The freedom found in letting go and surrendering to the flow of life*............................. 90

25. The Seven Blows. *The transformative power of adversity and the lessons learned through trials*............................. 94

26. The Moon and the Empty Sky. *The interconnectedness of all things and the vastness of the universe within*...................... 97

27. The Empty Mirror. *The nature of self-reflection and the realization of emptiness as liberation*............................. 100

28. The Bamboo Acrobat. *The balance between strength and flexibility in the pursuit of harmony.*................................ 104

29. The Empty Cup. *The openness and receptivity for spiritual growth and enlightenment.*... 108

30. The Old Ox. *The wisdom found in simplicity and the strength derived from inner peace.*.. 112

31. The Lost Horse. *Serendipity in misfortune, revealing life's unpredictable blessings.*.. 116

32. The Healing Waters. *Restoration and purity flowing from forgiveness and compassion.*....................................... 119

33. The Kind Baker. *The warmth of generosity transforming lives beyond mere sustenance.*.. 122

34. The Wise Crab. *Navigating challenges with strategy and insight overcomes brute force.*...................................... 126

35. The Four Guardians. *Unity and strength found in the diversity of protection.*... 129

36. The Laughing Buddha. *Joy and enlightenment in embracing the world as it is.*.. 133

37. The Courageous Mouse. *Small acts of bravery can lead to monumental changes.*.. 136

38. The Melody of Silence. *Discovering profound truths in the spaces between sounds.*.. 139

39. The Eternal Flame. *The undying light of wisdom that guides through generations.*.. 142

40. The Lost Compass. *Finding one's true path requires more than direction - it needs intuition.*............................... 146

41. The Magic Bowl. *Abundance and gratitude from what seems empty and minimal.*.. 150

42. The Bodhisattva and the Hungry Tigress. *Self-sacrifice as the ultimate act of compassion* 154

43. The Sacred Grove. *The sanctity of nature as a reflection of inner peace.* 157

44. The Golden Thread. *The interconnectedness of all lives woven through time.* 161

45. The Wise Gardener. *Cultivating growth through patience and persistent care.* 163

46. The Moonlit Path. *Illumination and clarity arriving in quiet, reflective moments.* 168

47. The Weaver's Daughter. *Weaving fate with the threads of diligence and faith.* 171

48. The Simile of the Saw. *Endurance and equanimity amidst life's severest tests.* 175

49. The Ten Bulls. *The stages of enlightenment unfolding in the quest for self-realization.* 179

50. The Wandering Cloud. *Freedom in detachment, flowing effortlessly with life's currents.* 183

51. The Laughing Monk. *Finding humor and wisdom amidst life's paradoxes.* 187

52. The Lotus Sutra. *The blossoming of universal enlightenment from the mud of earthly existence...* 191

Conclusion 195

Acknowledgements 198

The Mustard Seed

The potential for immense growth within the tiniest of beginnings.

In a bustling village nestled at the foot of a majestic mountain lived a young woman named Maya. Maya was known throughout the village for her radiant smile and kind heart, but beneath her cheerful exterior, she carried a heavy burden of sorrow.

Years ago, Maya had lost her beloved son in a tragic accident. The pain of his loss weighed heavily upon her, and she found herself consumed by grief each day. Try as she might, Maya could not shake the overwhelming sadness that clouded her spirit.

One day, desperate for solace, Maya sought out the wise old sage who lived on the outskirts of the village. She had heard tales of his profound wisdom and hoped that he might offer her some comfort.

Upon reaching the sage's humble abode, Maya poured out her heart, sharing the depths of her sorrow and despair. The sage listened patiently to her tale, his eyes filled with compassion.

"My dear child," the sage said softly, "I understand the pain you carry, but know that you are not alone in your suffering. Every person you encounter carries their own burden of sorrow, just as you do."

Maya was taken aback by his words. "But how can that be?" she asked incredulously. "Surely no one else knows the depth of my pain."

The sage nodded knowingly. "It is true that each person's pain is unique, but we are all bound together by the universal experience of suffering. Just as you grieve for your son, others grieve for their loved ones lost, their dreams unfulfilled, their hearts broken."

Seeing the doubt in Maya's eyes, the sage continued, "While each sorrow is unique, the experience of suffering unites us all. Allow me to show you the truth of my words. Take this mustard seed and journey through the village. Offer it only from households untouched by sorrow."

Maya accepted the mustard seed, still skeptical of the sage's teachings. Nevertheless, she set out on her journey, determined to prove him wrong.

As Maya knocked on door after door, she was met with sympathy and understanding from those who shared their own stories of loss and pain. From the wealthiest mansion to the humblest cottage, not a single household was untouched by sorrow.

With each encounter, Maya's heart softened, and she began to see the interconnectedness of all beings through their shared experiences of joy and suffering. Finally, as the sun dipped below the horizon, Maya returned to the sage's dwelling, tears of gratitude streaming down her cheeks.

"I understand now," she whispered, clutching the mustard seed tightly in her hand. "Thank you for showing me that I am not alone in my pain."

The sage smiled gently, his eyes twinkling with wisdom. "Maya, my child, the mustard seed you hold in your hand is a symbol of the universal truth: that all beings are bound together by the thread of suffering and the possibility of healing. Embrace this truth, and you will find the strength to carry on, knowing that you are never truly alone."

Reflection:

How often do we feel isolated in our pain, believing that we are the only ones facing challenges or experiencing sorrow? Maya's journey reminds us that suffering is a fundamental aspect of the human condition, transcending boundaries of age, race, and socioeconomic status. No one is immune to the trials and tribulations of life, and in recognizing this shared experience, we find solace in our common humanity.

Maya's willingness to listen to the stories of others and to open her heart to empathy and understanding serves as a powerful example for us all. In a world fraught with division and discord, cultivating compassion and connection is more important than ever. By acknowledging and honoring the suffering of others, we create space for healing and transformation, both within ourselves and within our communities.

The mustard seed that Maya holds in her hand symbolizes not only the universality of suffering but also the potential for growth and renewal that arises from acknowledging our shared humanity. Just as a tiny seed has the power to blossom into a mighty tree, so too does the recognition of our interconnectedness pave the way for compassion, resilience, and healing to take root in our lives.

Maya's journey reminds us that while suffering may be inevitable, it is not insurmountable. By embracing the truth of our interconnectedness and offering kindness and support to those around us, we can navigate life's challenges with grace and courage. As we reflect on Maya's story, may we be inspired to cultivate empathy, foster connection, and walk the path of healing and transformation together.

The Blind Men and the Elephant

The subjective nature of perception and the importance of holistic understanding.

In a small village nestled amidst rolling hills and lush forests, there lived six blind men who had heard tales of an extraordinary creature known as an elephant. Intrigued by the stories they had heard, the blind men set out on a journey to discover the truth for themselves.

As they traveled through the countryside, guided by the whispers of the wind and the warmth of the sun, the blind men relied on their other senses to navigate the world around them. With each step they took, they listened intently to the rustling of the leaves, the chirping of the birds, and the gentle flow of the nearby river.

After many days of travel, the blind men finally arrived at the outskirts of a bustling marketplace, where they heard rumors of an elephant that resided in the nearby forest. Eager to experience the wonder of the creature for themselves, the blind men set off towards the forest, their hearts filled with anticipation and excitement.

When they finally encountered the elephant, each man reached out to touch it, eager to understand its true nature. But as they explored the creature with their hands, they came to wildly different conclusions about its appearance and form.

The first blind man, who touched the elephant's trunk, declared that it was like a thick, sturdy tree trunk, strong and unyielding.

The second blind man, who felt its ear, argued that the elephant was like a large fan, flapping gently in the breeze.

The third blind man, who touched its tusk, insisted that the elephant was like a sharp, pointed spear, capable of piercing through any obstacle.

The fourth blind man, who felt its side, proclaimed that the elephant was like a massive wall, solid and impenetrable.

The fifth blind man, who touched its leg, exclaimed that the elephant was like a sturdy pillar, supporting the weight of the world with ease.

And the sixth blind man, who felt its tail, declared that the elephant was like a thick, coiled rope, strong and flexible.

And so, the blind men continued to argue, each convinced that their own perception of the elephant was the correct one. But in their blindness, they failed to see the truth—that the elephant was far greater than the sum of its parts, and that each of them held only a fragment of the whole.

As the blind men debated amongst themselves, a wise sage approached them, his eyes twinkling with amusement. He listened patiently to their arguments, then gently invited them to consider the possibility that they were all correct—and yet, they were also all wrong.

For, he explained, the nature of the elephant could not be fully understood by any single perspective alone. It was only by combining their diverse experiences and insights that they could begin to grasp the true essence of the creature.

With this wisdom in mind, the blind men paused their arguments and opened their hearts and minds to each other's perspectives. And as they shared their experiences and listened to one another with compassion and understanding, they began to see the elephant not as a collection of disparate parts, but as a majestic and awe-inspiring creature that transcended the limitations of their individual perceptions.

And in that moment of shared understanding, the blind men realized that true wisdom could only be found in humility and open-mindedness, and that by embracing the diversity of human experience, they could unlock the secrets of the universe and discover the interconnectedness of all things.

Reflection:

"The Blind Men and the Elephant" presents a timeless allegory that encourages us to consider the limitations of our individual perspectives and the importance of embracing diversity and open-mindedness in our pursuit of truth and understanding.

In our daily lives, we often encounter situations where our perceptions are limited by our own experiences, biases, and preconceptions. Like the blind men in the story, we may be quick to judge based on our own narrow viewpoints, failing to recognize the broader truth that lies beyond our immediate perceptions.

The blind men's differing interpretations of the elephant serve as a powerful reminder of the subjective nature of truth. Each man perceives the elephant based on his own unique encounter with a single aspect of the creature, leading to wildly different conclusions about its nature.

However, it is only when they come together and share their experiences that they begin to grasp the full complexity and richness of the elephant's existence. Through dialogue and collaboration, they are able to piece together a more holistic understanding of the creature, recognizing that each perspective offers valuable insights into its true essence.

This story prompts us to reflect on the importance of humility and open-mindedness in our interactions with others. It teaches us to approach differences in perception with curiosity and respect, acknowledging that there is often more than one valid interpretation of a given situation.

Ultimately, this story reminds us that true wisdom is not found in clinging rigidly to our own viewpoints, but in remaining open to the perspectives of others and embracing the complexity and diversity of human experience. By doing so, we can cultivate a deeper appreciation for the interconnectedness of all things and move closer towards a more inclusive and compassionate understanding of the world.

The Two Monks and the Woman

The consequences of judgment and liberation found in forgiveness.

In a tranquil monastery nestled amidst serene mountains and whispering pines, two monks, Aiden and Kaito, resided in quiet contemplation of the teachings of their order. Aiden, the elder monk, was revered for his wisdom and serenity, while Kaito, his younger companion, possessed a fervent zeal for spiritual practice.

One day, as the monks embarked on their journey to a neighboring village to collect alms, they came upon a rushing river swollen with rainwater from the recent storm. At the water's edge stood a young woman dressed in fine silk robes, her eyes filled with fear as she hesitated to cross the swollen torrent.

Without a moment's hesitation, Aiden approached the woman and offered to carry her across the river on his back. Gratefully, she accepted his offer, and with practiced ease, Aiden lifted her into his arms and waded through the rushing waters to the other side.

As they reached the safety of the riverbank, the woman thanked Aiden profusely and continued on her way, disappearing into the distance. With a serene smile, Aiden rejoined Kaito, and together they resumed their journey to the village, their hearts lightened by the knowledge that they had helped someone in need.

Hours passed, and the sun began to sink below the horizon as the monks made their way back to the monastery. Along the path, Kaito turned to Aiden with a troubled expression, his mind filled with questions.

"Brother Aiden," Kaito began hesitantly, "I cannot help but wonder—why did you carry that woman across the river? Our order forbids us from touching women, yet you willingly broke this rule without hesitation. I do not understand."

Aiden listened patiently to Kaito's words, his eyes filled with compassion for his young companion's confusion. With a gentle smile, he offered Kaito a simple yet profound response.

"My dear brother," Aiden said softly, "when I carried the woman across the river, I did so out of compassion and a desire to alleviate her suffering. In that moment, there was no 'woman' or 'monk'—there was only a fellow being in need of help. The river does not distinguish between men and women, and neither should we."

With these words, Aiden continued on his way, leaving Kaito to ponder the wisdom of his words as they journeyed back to the monastery in silence.

Days turned into weeks, and weeks into months, but the encounter with the woman by the river lingered in Kaito's mind like a gentle whisper in the wind. With each passing day, he found himself reflecting on Aiden's words and the profound lesson they held for him.

And as he meditated on the teachings of his wise elder, Kaito came to understand the true meaning of compassion and the importance of seeing beyond the labels and distinctions that divide us. In the eyes of compassion, there is no 'self' or 'other'—there is only the boundless expanse of the human heart, reaching out to embrace all beings with love and understanding.

Reflection:

"The Two Monks and the Woman" offers a profound meditation on the nature of compassion and the limitations of rigid rules and conventions. Through Aiden's simple yet profound act of kindness, we are reminded of the importance of seeing beyond labels and distinctions to recognize the shared humanity that unites us all.

In reflecting on the story, we are invited to consider the ways in which our own perceptions and beliefs may limit our capacity for compassion and understanding. Like Kaito, we may find ourselves bound by the constraints of rigid rules and conventions, unable to see the deeper truth that lies beyond.

"The Two Monks and the Woman" challenges us to break free from the limitations of our own minds and embrace the boundless expanse of the human heart. In the eyes of compassion, there are no barriers or distinctions—only the pure, unbounded love that transcends all differences and unites us in a shared journey of healing and transformation.

May we heed the wisdom of Aiden and Kaito, and strive to cultivate compassion in our own lives, seeing beyond the surface of appearances to recognize the inherent dignity and worth of all beings. For in embracing the true spirit of compassion, we discover the path to greater peace, joy, and fulfillment for ourselves and for all beings.

The Tiger and the Strawberry

*The power of presence and finding joy in
the simplicity of life.*

In the heart of a dense forest, where ancient trees towered overhead and shafts of sunlight filtered through the canopy, there dwelled a solitary monk named Tenzin. With his weathered robes and serene countenance, Tenzin moved through the forest with quiet reverence, his footsteps light upon the earth.

One tranquil morning, as Tenzin followed a winding path through the forest, he stumbled upon a scene that stopped him in his tracks—a magnificent tiger, its sleek fur matted and tangled in a crude snare. The tiger's amber eyes blazed with fury and fear, its powerful form thrashing against the confines of the trap.

Tenzin approached the trapped tiger with caution, his heart heavy with compassion. Drawing upon the teachings of his faith, he knelt beside the trembling animal and spoke softly, his voice a soothing melody amidst the chaos of the forest.

"Fierce one," Tenzin said, "I mean you no harm. Let me help you."

With steady hands and a gentle touch, Tenzin set to work unraveling the twisted strands of the snare, his fingers deftly navigating the intricate knots. As he worked, he whispered words of comfort to the tiger, offering reassurance and solace in the midst of its suffering.

Gradually, the tension in the tiger's body began to ease, and its fierce gaze softened into one of gratitude. With a final tug, Tenzin freed the majestic creature from its bonds, watching as it bounded off into the forest, a blur of orange and black against the greenery.

Alone once more in the clearing, Tenzin felt a profound sense of peace settle over him—a quiet knowing that he had made a difference in the life of another being. But even as he reveled in this small victory, he was reminded of the impermanence of all things—a truth that echoed through the rustle of leaves and the whisper of the wind.

Continuing on his journey, Tenzin soon found himself standing at the edge of a steep cliff, overlooking a rushing river below. Perched precariously on the edge of the precipice, a single ripe strawberry dangled temptingly within reach, its crimson hue a vivid contrast against the verdant landscape.

Without hesitation, Tenzin reached out and plucked the strawberry from its stem, cradling it gently in the palm of his hand. Bringing it to his lips, he closed his eyes and savored the sweetness of its flesh, allowing the tangy juice to dance across his tongue in a symphony of flavor.

In that fleeting moment, as the sun dipped low on the horizon and the forest around him hummed with the song of life, Tenzin experienced a profound sense of gratitude and joy. For in the simple act of tasting the strawberry, he found a glimpse of the divine—a reminder of the boundless beauty and wonder that permeated the world, even in the face of darkness and despair.

Reflection:

The tale of the tiger and the strawberry is a testament to the transformative power of compassion, mindfulness, and gratitude. Tenzin's act of kindness towards the trapped tiger illustrates the profound impact that a single act of compassion can have, not only on the recipient but also on the giver. By extending empathy and care to those in need, we create a ripple effect of healing and kindness that reverberates throughout the world.

Likewise, Tenzin's decision to savor the strawberry represents a shift in perspective—a recognition of the inherent beauty and richness of life, even amidst its trials and tribulations. In embracing the present moment with openness and appreciation, we discover that true happiness arises not from external circumstances but from within.

As we reflect on Tenzin's story, may we be inspired to cultivate compassion, mindfulness, and gratitude in our own lives. May we extend a helping hand to those in need, savoring each moment with awareness and appreciation, knowing that every act of kindness and every moment of joy is a precious gift to be cherished.

The Stonecutter

The journey of self-discovery and the realization of inner strength.

In a distant village nestled among towering mountains, there lived a humble stonecutter named Koji. From dawn till dusk, Koji toiled away in the quarries, chiseling and shaping blocks of stone with skill and precision. Despite his laborious work, Koji found contentment in his craft, taking pride in the beauty and strength of the stones he sculpted.

One scorching summer day, as Koji labored beneath the sweltering sun, he caught sight of a procession passing through the village—a grand entourage of noblemen and courtiers, led by a powerful lord adorned in resplendent robes and jewels. Mesmerized by the spectacle, Koji watched as the procession made its way towards the lord's lavish palace, its walls gleaming with opulence and grandeur.

As Koji gazed upon the magnificent palace, a seed of longing took root in his heart—a yearning for wealth and power beyond his humble station. Envious of the lord's riches and prestige, Koji wished fervently to trade places with him, to bask in the adulation of the masses and command the respect of all who beheld him.

To his astonishment, Koji's wish was granted, and in an instant, he found himself transformed into the lord of the palace, his rough garments replaced by robes of silk and satin, his calloused hands adorned with jewels and gold. Thrilled by his newfound status, Koji reveled in the adulation of his subjects, relishing the power and prestige that now lay within his grasp.

But as the days passed and Koji grew accustomed to his life of luxury, a sense of disillusionment began to creep into his heart. Despite his wealth and power, he found himself plagued by worries and anxieties, his days consumed by the relentless pursuit of ever-greater riches and influence.

One evening, as Koji sat alone in his opulent chamber, gazing out at the moonlit sky, he heard a soft voice whispering in the darkness—a voice that spoke of the futility of worldly desires and the fleeting nature of human existence.

Startled by the voice, Koji turned to see a wise old monk standing before him, his eyes filled with compassion and wisdom. With gentle words, the monk reminded Koji of the simple joys and pleasures that he had once known as a humble stonecutter—the feel of the cool breeze upon his face, the warmth of the sun upon his back, the satisfaction of creating something of beauty and value with his own hands.

Moved by the monk's words, Koji realized the folly of his desires and the emptiness of his pursuit of wealth and power. With a heavy heart, he begged the monk to undo the wish that had brought him such fleeting happiness, longing once more for the simple life of a stonecutter.

In an instant, Koji found himself back in the quarries, his hands gripping the rough-hewn stone with renewed purpose and determination. Though he had returned to his former life, Koji felt a profound sense of peace and contentment settle over him, knowing that true happiness could be found not in wealth or power, but in the simplicity of living in harmony with the natural world.

And so, Koji continued to work as a stonecutter, finding joy and fulfillment in the beauty of his craft and the serenity of the mountains that surrounded him, his heart forever grateful for the wisdom that had guided him back to the path of contentment and inner peace.

Reflection:

"The Stonecutter" is a poignant reminder of the dangers of pursuing worldly desires at the expense of inner contentment and spiritual fulfillment. Through Koji's journey, we witness the allure of wealth and power and the emptiness that accompanies their attainment. Yet, we also see the transformative power of wisdom and self-awareness in guiding us back to a life of simplicity and authenticity.

Koji's longing for the trappings of wealth and status reflects a universal desire for recognition and validation, but his eventual disillusionment serves as a cautionary tale about the fleeting nature of worldly success. In our own lives, we may find ourselves tempted by the allure of material wealth, social status, or external validation, but true fulfillment can only be found by aligning our actions with our deepest values and aspirations.

The wise old monk who appears to Koji represents the voice of inner wisdom, gently guiding him back to the path of contentment and inner peace. Through his teachings, we are reminded of the importance of cultivating mindfulness, gratitude, and self-awareness in our lives, and the transformative power of letting go of attachments to external markers of success.

As we reflect on Koji's story, may we be inspired to examine our own desires and aspirations, and to seek fulfillment not in the pursuit of wealth or power, but in the simple joys of everyday life.

May we cultivate a sense of gratitude for the blessings that surround us, and strive to live with integrity and authenticity, knowing that true happiness lies not in what we possess, but in who we are.

The Four Wives

The multifaceted nature of love and the depth of human relationships.

In a bustling village nestled amidst verdant hills, there lived a wealthy merchant named Raj. Though blessed with abundant wealth and prosperity, Raj found himself plagued by a sense of discontentment that gnawed at his heart like a persistent ache. Despite his material riches, Raj felt a profound emptiness within him—a void that no amount of wealth or possessions could fill.

One day, as Raj wandered the streets of the village lost in thought, he came upon an old sage seated beneath the shade of a towering banyan tree. Drawn to the sage's serene countenance, Raj approached him with a sense of longing in his heart, hoping to find solace in the sage's wisdom.

"What troubles you, my son?" the sage asked kindly, his eyes twinkling with compassion.

Raj sighed heavily, pouring out his heart to the sage, confessing his feelings of discontentment and longing for true happiness.

The sage listened patiently to Raj's tale, nodding in understanding. "I believe I can offer you some guidance," he said gently. "But first, allow me to tell you a story—a story of four wives."

Intrigued, Raj settled himself at the sage's feet, eager to hear the tale.

The Tale of the Four Wives

Once upon a time, in a distant kingdom, there lived a wealthy merchant much like yourself, Raj. This merchant, too, was plagued by feelings of discontentment and longing for true happiness. So, he sought the counsel of a wise sage, who shared with him the tale of the four wives.

The first wife, the sage explained, was a beautiful and elegant woman who captivated the merchant with her grace and charm. She was a faithful companion, accompanying him to social gatherings and lavish banquets, but she was also vain and self-absorbed, caring only for her own beauty and status.

The second wife, the sage continued, was a devoted and loving partner who stood by the merchant's side through thick and thin. She shared his joys and sorrows, offering comfort and support in times of need, but she was also possessive and jealous, demanding his undivided attention and affection.

The third wife, the sage went on, was a skilled and resourceful woman who managed the merchant's household with efficiency and diligence. She ensured that his every need was met, from the finest meals to the most luxurious comforts, but she was also ambitious, always seeking to climb higher on the social ladder and acquire more wealth and power.

Finally, the sage revealed, there was the fourth wife—a quiet and unassuming woman who lived in the shadows, unnoticed and overlooked by all. She spoke little and asked for nothing, content to serve the merchant with humility and devotion, but she was also wise and insightful, possessing a deep understanding of the true nature of happiness and fulfillment.

As Raj listened to the sage's tale, he felt a sense of recognition stir within him—a recognition of the different aspects of himself reflected in the four wives. Like the merchant in the story, Raj realized that he had been seeking happiness and fulfillment in external sources—wealth, status, and possessions—only to find himself still longing for something more.

The first wife represented Raj's desire for beauty and pleasure, the second his need for love and companionship, and the third his quest for success and achievement. But it was the fourth wife—the quiet, unassuming one—who held the key to true happiness, reminding Raj of the importance of inner contentment and spiritual fulfillment.

Inspired by the sage's wisdom, Raj resolved to embrace the lessons of the four wives and to live his life with greater mindfulness and authenticity. No longer would he be driven by the pursuit of wealth or status, but by a deep sense of purpose and meaning that transcended the boundaries of the material world.

He realized that true happiness could not be found in material possessions or external achievements, but in cultivating a sense of gratitude, compassion, and inner peace.

The Reflection:

"The Four Wives" serves as a poignant reminder of the complexities of human desire and the quest for true happiness. Through the allegory of the four wives, we are invited to reflect on the different facets of our own lives and the myriad desires that drive us.

Like the merchant in the story, we may find ourselves seeking fulfillment in external sources—whether it be wealth, success, or love—only to discover that true happiness remains elusive. The first wife represents our longing for beauty and pleasure, the second our need for love and companionship, and the third our pursuit of success and achievement. Yet, it is the fourth wife—the quiet, unassuming one—who holds the key to true contentment, reminding us of the importance of inner peace and spiritual fulfillment.

As we contemplate the sage's words, we are reminded of the fleeting nature of worldly desires and the impermanence of external possessions. True happiness, we come to realize, cannot be found in material wealth or external achievements, but in cultivating a sense of gratitude, compassion, and inner peace within ourselves.

Inspired by the wisdom of the four wives, we are called to live our lives with greater mindfulness and authenticity, seeking fulfillment not in what we possess, but in who we are. By embracing the lessons of humility, gratitude, and compassion, we can find joy and contentment in the simple pleasures of everyday life, knowing that true happiness lies not in what we have, but in how we live.

As we journey through life, may we be guided by the timeless wisdom of the four wives, finding fulfillment in acts of kindness and compassion, and embracing the richness of the present moment with open hearts and grateful spirits.

The Lost Sutra Scroll

The enduring presence of wisdom, waiting to be unveiled.

In the heart of a verdant forest, where ancient trees whispered secrets to the wind and streams murmured melodies of bygone days, there stood a secluded temple known as the Sanctuary of Eternal Wisdom. Within its hallowed halls, monks devoted themselves to the study of ancient scriptures and the pursuit of enlightenment.

Legend had it that nestled within the depths of the temple library lay a sacred sutra scroll—a priceless treasure said to contain the wisdom of the ages. Written by the hand of a revered sage centuries ago, the scroll was believed to hold the key to unlocking the mysteries of existence and attaining spiritual liberation.

For generations, the monks of the Sanctuary had safeguarded the precious scroll, passing down its teachings from one generation to the next. Yet, despite their best efforts, the whereabouts of the scroll had become lost to time, its existence known only through the whispers of legend and lore.

One fateful day, a young novice named Tenzin stumbled upon an ancient manuscript hidden within the recesses of the temple library.

As he dusted off the weathered pages and deciphered the cryptic script, he realized with a start that he had uncovered the long-lost sutra scroll—the very treasure that had eluded the monks for centuries.

Eager to share his discovery with his fellow monks, Tenzin rushed to the temple courtyard, where the elders were gathered in quiet contemplation. With trembling hands, he unfurled the scroll before them, revealing its sacred teachings to the astonished assembly.

As the monks studied the ancient text, their hearts filled with reverence and awe. Here, in the words of the sage, lay the timeless wisdom of the Buddha—the path to enlightenment laid bare for all who sought it.

But even as the monks marveled at the beauty of the sutra scroll, a shadow fell across the temple grounds—a dark omen of impending danger. For word of the scroll's discovery had spread far and wide, reaching the ears of a band of ruthless bandits who coveted its priceless secrets.

Driven by greed and lust for power, the bandits descended upon the Sanctuary under the cover of night, their weapons gleaming in the moonlight as they laid siege to the temple walls. With cries of rage and defiance, the monks rallied to defend their sacred home, determined to protect the precious scroll at all costs.

In the midst of the chaos and confusion, Tenzin seized the opportunity to slip away unnoticed, clutching the sutra scroll to his chest as he fled into the darkness of the forest. With each step, he felt the weight of responsibility pressing down upon him—the fate of the scroll and the future of the temple resting squarely on his shoulders.

For days and nights, Tenzin wandered through the dense undergrowth, guided only by the light of the stars and the whispers of the wind. At last, weary and exhausted, he stumbled upon a hidden cave deep within the heart of the forest—a sanctuary of solitude where he could safeguard the scroll from harm.

And there, in the quiet stillness of the cave, Tenzin vowed to preserve the wisdom of the sutra scroll for future generations, ensuring that its teachings would endure for all time. And though the world outside may be engulfed in chaos and strife, within the sanctuary of his heart, the light of the ancient wisdom shone bright, illuminating the path to enlightenment for all who sought it.

Reflection:

The tale of the Lost Sutra Scroll is a captivating narrative that prompts reflection on the timeless themes of wisdom, courage, and sacrifice.

At its core, the story underscores the significance of knowledge and enlightenment in the pursuit of spiritual growth. The discovery of the ancient scroll within the temple library symbolizes the quest for deeper understanding and the preservation of wisdom through the ages. It serves as a reminder of the enduring value of ancient teachings and the profound impact they can have on those who encounter them.

The actions of Tenzin, the young novice who uncovers the scroll, exemplify the virtues of bravery and selflessness. Despite the imminent danger posed by the bandits, Tenzin risks his own safety to safeguard the sacred text, recognizing the importance of protecting the scroll's teachings for the greater good. His decision to flee into the forest and seek refuge in a hidden cave reflects a deep sense of responsibility and devotion to preserving the scroll's wisdom for future generations.

As we reflect on the tale of the Lost Sutra Scroll, we are reminded of the profound impact that knowledge and enlightenment can have on individuals and communities alike. It prompts us to consider the significance of preserving ancient wisdom and passing it down through generations, ensuring that the teachings of the past continue to inspire and guide us in the present.

In essence, the tale of the Lost Sutra Scroll is a timeless narrative inviting us to reflect on the enduring power of wisdom, the importance of bravery in the face of adversity, and the profound impact that individuals can have on the course of history.

The Elephant Rope

The breaking free from self-imposed limitations and realizing true potential.

In the heart of a bustling village, nestled amidst emerald forests and rolling hills, lived a young boy named Raju. Raju was a curious soul, his eyes filled with wonder at the world around him. Every day, he ventured into the village marketplace, eager to explore and learn from the sights and sounds that surrounded him.

One day, as Raju wandered through the marketplace, he came upon a group of majestic elephants tethered to sturdy posts with thick ropes. The elephants towered over the crowd, their powerful frames and wise eyes captivating Raju's attention. Despite their immense size and strength, the elephants stood motionless, their mighty bodies held captive by the flimsy constraints of the ropes.

Intrigued by what he saw, Raju approached one of the elephants and gently reached out to touch its rough, wrinkled skin. He could feel the warmth of the elephant's breath as it gazed down at him with eyes that seemed to hold ancient wisdom.

Curious, Raju turned to a passing trainer and asked why the elephants did not break free from their bonds. The trainer chuckled at the boy's question and explained that when the elephants were young, they were tied to similar ropes that they were too weak to break. As they grew older, the elephants never realized their own strength, and the belief that they were still bound by the ropes persisted in their minds.

As Raju listened to the trainer's words, a spark ignited within him—a spark of curiosity and determination to free the elephants from their mental chains. With each passing day, he returned to the marketplace, spending hours observing and studying the elephants, seeking to understand their behavior and unlock the secrets of their captivity.

And then, one day, as Raju stood amidst the elephants, a thought occurred to him—a simple yet profound realization that would change everything. He realized that the elephants were not truly bound by the ropes, but by the limitations of their own minds—that their belief in their inability to break free was the only thing holding them back.

With newfound purpose and determination, Raju set out to challenge the elephants' perceptions and help them see the truth—that they were no longer bound by the ropes that once held them captive. With patience and perseverance, he began to work with the animals, coaxing them to test their strength and challenge the limits of their perceived limitations.

Slowly but surely, the elephants began to realize the truth—that they were no longer bound by the ropes that once held them captive. With each tug and pull, they felt the bonds of their captivity loosen, until finally, they broke free from their constraints and roamed the village streets with a sense of liberation that filled the air with joy and wonder.

As Raju watched the elephants revel in their newfound freedom, he realized the power of belief and the importance of challenging the limitations that hold us back in life. Just like the elephants, he understood that we are often held captive by our own perceptions and beliefs, and that true freedom lies in recognizing the strength and potential that lies within us all.

Reflection:

"The Elephant Rope" serves as a poignant allegory for the limitations we impose upon ourselves through our beliefs and perceptions. Just as the elephants were held captive by the belief that they were still bound by the ropes of their youth, so too are we often held back by the limitations of our own minds.

In reflecting on the story, we are invited to consider the ways in which we may be limiting ourselves in our own lives, and to challenge the beliefs and perceptions that hold us back from reaching our full potential. By recognizing the strength and resilience that lies within us, we can break free from the mental chains that bind us and embrace a life of limitless possibility and opportunity.

"The Elephant Rope" reminds us that true freedom begins in the mind—that by shifting our perceptions and beliefs, we can unlock the door to a world of infinite potential and possibility. As we journey through life, may we remember the lesson of the elephants and embrace the power of belief to set us free from the constraints of our own making.

The Dog's Empty Dream

The nature of material pursuits and the search for true fulfillment.

In a small village nestled amidst rolling hills and golden fields, there lived a stray dog named Max. Abandoned by his owners and left to fend for himself, Max wandered the streets in search of food and shelter, his once bright eyes dulled by the hardships of life.

Despite his struggles, Max harbored a secret dream—a dream of finding a loving home where he would be cherished and cared for. Each night, as he curled up beneath the stars, he would close his eyes and imagine a place where he was no longer alone—a place where he was loved and wanted.

But as the days turned into weeks and the weeks into months, Max's dream began to fade, replaced by a sense of hopelessness and despair. He watched as families passed him by, their faces turned away in indifference, and he wondered if he would ever find the love and acceptance he so desperately craved.

One day, as Max wandered through the village square, he came upon a kind-hearted couple sitting on a bench, their arms outstretched in welcome. With trembling paws, Max approached them, his heart pounding with fear and anticipation.

To his surprise, the couple greeted him with open arms, their eyes filled with warmth and compassion. They offered Max a home—a place where he could find love and security, and where his dreams could finally become a reality.

Overwhelmed with gratitude, Max accepted their offer, his heart swelling with joy as he followed them to their cozy cottage on the edge of the village. And as he settled into his new home, surrounded by love and kindness, Max realized that his dream had finally come true—that in the embrace of his new family, he had found the happiness and belonging he had always longed for.

Days turned into weeks, and weeks into months, as Max reveled in the love and warmth of his new family. Each day brought new adventures and experiences, as Max explored the world around him with the boundless energy and enthusiasm of a puppy.

But amidst the joy and laughter, Max never forgot the struggles he had faced as a stray—a reminder of the countless other animals who still roamed the streets in search of love and acceptance. And so, with a heart filled with compassion, Max resolved to pay forward the kindness he had received by helping others in need.

With the support of his loving family, Max embarked on a mission to make a difference in the lives of stray animals across the village. Together, they provided food, shelter, and medical care to those in need, offering a second chance at life to those who had been forgotten and neglected.

And as Max looked upon the faces of his furry friends, he knew that his dream had not only come true for himself, but for countless others as well. In the embrace of love and compassion, Max had found not only a home, but a purpose—a purpose to make the world a better place, one act of kindness at a time.

As Max curled up beside his loving family each night, he closed his eyes with a sense of peace and contentment, knowing that he had finally found his place in the world—a place where love knew no bounds, and dreams had the power to come true.

Reflections:

"The Dog's Empty Dream" presents a poignant narrative that speaks to the universal themes of hope, resilience, and the transformative power of love. Through Max's journey from a lonely stray to a cherished member of a loving family, we are reminded of the inherent capacity for growth and transformation that lies within each of us.

Max's experience serves as a testament to the resilience of the human spirit, demonstrating that even in the face of seemingly insurmountable obstacles, hope can endure. Despite the challenges he faced as a stray dog, Max never lost sight of his dream of finding a loving home—a dream that sustained him through the darkest of times.

Max's story underscores the transformative power of love and acceptance. It is through the kindness and compassion of others that Max is able to find a sense of belonging and fulfillment, ultimately realizing his dream of finding a loving home. In a world often marked by division and strife, Max's journey serves as a powerful reminder of the importance of extending empathy and compassion to those in need.

The Three Questions

The pursuit of wisdom and self-discovery through introspection.

In a kingdom ruled by a wise and just king, there lived a young prince named Leo. Despite his privileged upbringing, Leo possessed a restless spirit and a burning desire to unlock the secrets of life and death.

One day, as he wandered through the palace gardens, Leo came upon a wise hermit meditating beneath the shade of a towering oak tree. Intrigued by the hermit's serene demeanor, Leo approached him with a question burning in his heart.

"Tell me, wise one," Leo asked eagerly, "what is the most important time? What is the right thing to do? And who is the most important person?"

The hermit listened patiently to Leo's questions, his eyes twinkling with wisdom as he pondered the prince's words. And then, with a gentle smile, he offered Leo three simple yet profound answers.

"The most important time," the hermit said, "is now. The past is gone, and the future is yet to come. All we have is this moment, and it is up to us to make the most of it."

"The right thing to do," he continued, "is to do good whenever we can. In every action, large or small, we have the opportunity to make a positive difference in the world and leave a lasting legacy of kindness and compassion."

"And as for the most important person," the hermit concluded, "it is the one who is standing before you. Every person we encounter is deserving of our respect and attention, for each one carries within them the spark of divinity and the potential to change the world."

With these words, the hermit fell silent, his gaze fixed upon Leo with a look of profound understanding.

As the prince reflected on the hermit's answers, he realized that the secrets of life and death were not found in distant lands or hidden truths, but in the simple wisdom of the present moment and the power of love and compassion to transform the world. With gratitude in his heart, he bowed deeply to the wise hermit before taking his leave, his mind buzzing with thoughts of how he could apply these timeless truths to his own life.

Determined to put the hermit's wisdom into practice, Prince Leo returned to the palace with a renewed sense of purpose. He sought out his father, the king, eager to share the hermit's teachings and discuss how they could be integrated into the kingdom's governance.

With his father's blessing, Prince Leo embarked on a journey across the kingdom, spreading the message of compassion, kindness, and mindfulness to all who would listen. He visited towns and villages, speaking to farmers, merchants, and artisans, and sharing the hermit's wisdom with all who crossed his path.

Along the way, Prince Leo encountered individuals from all walks of life, each with their own struggles and challenges. From the humblest peasant to the wealthiest noble, he treated each person with the same kindness and respect, recognizing the divinity and potential within each soul.

And as he reflected on his own journey of growth and discovery, Prince Leo came to understand that true wisdom was not found in the answers to life's questions, but in the journey of seeking those answers with an open heart and a willingness to learn.

Reflections:

The encounter between Prince Leo and the wise hermit in "The Three Questions" offers profound insights into the nature of existence and the pursuit of wisdom. Through the hermit's simple yet profound answers, we are reminded of the timeless truths that shape our understanding of the world and our place within it.

The hermit's first answer, that the most important time is now, serves as a powerful reminder of the significance of living in the present moment. In a world often consumed by regrets of the past or anxieties about the future, we are reminded of the importance of embracing the present moment and making the most of the opportunities it offers.

Similarly, the hermit's second answer, emphasizing the importance of doing good whenever we can, highlights the transformative power of kindness and compassion. In a world filled with challenges and uncertainties, we are reminded that even the smallest acts of kindness can have a profound impact on the lives of others and contribute to the greater good.

Finally, the hermit's assertion that the most important person is the one who is standing before us underscores the importance of recognizing the inherent dignity and worth of every individual. In a world often marked by division and discord, we are reminded of the importance of treating others with respect and compassion, regardless of their background or circumstances.

In reflecting on "The Three Questions," we are invited to consider how we can apply these timeless truths to our own lives. By embracing the present moment, cultivating kindness and compassion, and recognizing the inherent value of every individual, we can navigate the complexities of life with wisdom, grace, and humility.

The Golden Fish

The fleeting nature of desire and the true riches found within.

In a quaint fishing village nestled along the shimmering shores of a crystal-clear lake, there lived a humble fisherman named Hiro. From the break of dawn until the setting of the sun, Hiro could be found plying his trade, casting his nets into the tranquil waters in hopes of a bountiful catch to provide for his family.

Despite his unwavering dedication to his craft, Hiro's fortunes had dwindled in recent months. The once abundant waters had grown increasingly sparse, leaving Hiro with meager catches barely enough to sustain his family's needs. Desperate to find a solution, Hiro ventured farther out into the lake each day, casting his nets with renewed determination in search of a miracle.

One morning, as Hiro was preparing to cast his nets, he spotted something glimmering beneath the surface of the water. Curious, he leaned closer and was astonished to see a radiant golden fish swimming gracefully in the depths below. Its scales shimmered like the sun's rays dancing upon the water, and its eyes sparkled with an otherworldly brilliance.

Filled with wonder and awe, Hiro reached out his hand and gently caught the golden fish in his net. But as he held the shimmering creature in his hands, he hesitated, struck by the fish's beauty and grace.

"Please, kind fisherman," the golden fish spoke in a voice as melodious as a songbird's, "release me back into the waters, and I will grant you a wish as a token of my gratitude."

Hiro's heart skipped a beat at the fish's words, his mind racing with possibilities. For a moment, he considered wealth and riches beyond his wildest dreams. But as he looked into the fish's eyes, he saw not greed, but a profound sense of compassion and wisdom.

With a solemn nod, Hiro carefully lowered the golden fish back into the cool embrace of the lake.

"Thank you, noble fish," Hiro said with a bow, "for your generous offer. If it pleases you, I wish for nothing more than the health and happiness of my family."

With a flick of its tail, the golden fish vanished beneath the waves, leaving Hiro standing on the shore with a heart full of gratitude and hope.

Days turned into weeks, and weeks into months, as Hiro continued his life as a humble fisherman. And though he often wondered if the golden fish's promise had been nothing more than a dream, he never forgot the profound sense of peace and contentment that had washed over him in that moment.

As time passed, Hiro's fortunes began to change. The waters of the lake teemed with life once more, providing Hiro with an abundance of fish beyond his wildest dreams. With each catch, Hiro felt a sense of gratitude and humility, knowing that his family's needs were provided for through the generosity of the lake and its inhabitants.

Years passed, and Hiro's family flourished under his care, their days filled with laughter, love, and simple joys. And as Hiro looked upon the smiling faces of his children and grandchildren, he knew that his greatest wish had already been granted—a life filled with love, laughter, and cherished memories.

And though the golden fish had long since disappeared beneath the waves, Hiro carried its gift with him always—a reminder that true wealth lies not in material possessions, but in the love and happiness we share with those we hold dear.

As the years went by, Hiro's story spread far and wide, becoming a legend among the villagers who marveled at the fisherman's good fortune. And though some dismissed it as mere superstition, others saw in Hiro's tale a timeless reminder of the power of gratitude, kindness, and the simple joys of life.

And so, as the sun set upon another day in the fishing village, Hiro cast his nets into the shimmering waters once more, his heart overflowing with gratitude for the blessings he had received and the simple joys of life that awaited him with each new dawn.

Reflections:

"The Golden Fish" offers a timeless tale of gratitude, generosity, and the true meaning of wealth. Through Hiro's encounter with the golden fish, we are reminded of the importance of humility and gratitude in the face of unexpected blessings.

In reflecting on this story, we are invited to consider the ways in which we can cultivate a spirit of gratitude in our own lives. Like Hiro, we may encounter moments of unexpected kindness and generosity that leave a lasting impression on our hearts. By acknowledging these gifts with humility and gratitude, we open ourselves up to a deeper appreciation for the abundance that surrounds us.

Moreover, "The Golden Fish" challenges us to reconsider our notions of wealth and prosperity. In a world often defined by material possessions and external markers of success, Hiro's simple wish for the health and happiness of his family serves as a powerful reminder that true wealth lies not in what we own, but in the love and relationships we nurture.

As we contemplate Hiro's story, we are encouraged to reflect on the ways in which we can cultivate a sense of abundance in our own lives. Whether through acts of kindness and generosity towards others or by fostering deep and meaningful connections with our loved ones, we have the power to create a life filled with richness and meaning.

Ultimately, "The Golden Fish" reminds us that true wealth is not measured by the size of our bank accounts or the possessions we accumulate, but by the depth of our relationships and the love we share with those we hold dear. In embracing a spirit of gratitude and generosity, we discover the true abundance that lies within us all.

The Salt Doll

The dissolution of ego and the realization of oneness with the universe.

Once, in a distant land shrouded in mist and mystery, there stood a serene shoreline where the gentle waves of the ocean met the soft sands of the beach. On this beach, there lived a curious salt doll, formed from the grains of sand by the hand of the sea itself.

The salt doll had long pondered the mysteries of the world around it—the ebb and flow of the tides, the dance of the waves, and the vast expanse of the ocean stretching out to the horizon. Each day, it would sit upon the shore, gazing out at the shimmering waters with a sense of wonder and curiosity.

Driven by a deep yearning to understand the world beyond the shore, the salt doll resolved to venture out into the ocean, to explore the depths and unlock the secrets that lay hidden beneath the surface. With each step, it felt the cool, refreshing waters enveloping its form, dissolving the grains of sand that composed its body.

As the salt doll waded deeper into the ocean, it felt its essence gradually merging with the vastness of the sea. With each passing moment, its form began to soften and fade, until it was no longer a separate entity but a part of the ocean itself—a single drop in the boundless expanse of existence.

In its dissolution, the salt doll experienced a profound sense of liberation and expansion. No longer bound by the limitations of its individual form, it felt itself merging with the currents of the ocean, flowing effortlessly with the rhythm of the waves.

As it dissolved into the ocean, the salt doll became aware of the interconnectedness of all things—the rocks and the trees, the birds and the fish, the stars and the sky—all bound together in a vast web of existence. In that moment of realization, it understood that it was not separate from the world around it, but an integral part of it—a thread in the tapestry of creation.

And in that moment of unity, the salt doll found peace. It no longer felt the need to search for answers or understand its place in the world, for it knew that it was already home—in the embrace of the ocean, in the heart of existence itself.

As the waves gently lapped against the shore, the salt doll dissolved completely into the ocean, its essence merging with the waters that had given it life. And though its physical form had vanished, its presence lingered on in the gentle rhythm of the waves, in the whisper of the wind, in the shimmer of the stars overhead.

And so, the salt doll became one with the ocean, forever a part of the vast, boundless expanse of existence—a silent witness to the ever-changing dance of life and death, of creation and dissolution, of beginnings and endings. Discovering a profound sense of peace and serenity, knowing that it was not separate from the world around it, but an integral part of it—a single drop in the vast, boundless sea of existence.

Reflection:

"The Salt Doll" offers a poignant allegory for the journey of self-discovery and enlightenment. Through the story of the salt doll's dissolution into the ocean, we are invited to contemplate the nature of existence and the ultimate reality of interconnectedness.

At its core, the story speaks to the fundamental truth of oneness—the idea that all of creation is interconnected and interdependent, bound together by the invisible threads of existence. Like the salt doll dissolving into the ocean, we too are invited to let go of the illusion of separateness and recognize our inherent unity with all of life.

In reflecting on this story, we are challenged to consider the ways in which we can transcend the limitations of our individual selves and experience a deeper sense of connection with the world around us. By letting go of our attachments to ego and identity, we can open ourselves up to the vastness of existence and discover the peace and serenity that comes from realizing our true nature.

Ultimately, "The Salt Doll" reminds us that we are not separate from the world around us, but an integral part of it. In embracing the truth of our interconnectedness, we can find liberation from the suffering of the ego and experience a profound sense of unity and oneness with all of creation.

The Arrow Maker

The importance of purpose and direction in the journey of life.

In a tranquil village nestled amidst rolling hills and lush forests, there lived an elderly man named Hiroshi, renowned throughout the land as the finest arrow maker in all the kingdom. With weathered hands and keen eyes, Hiroshi crafted each arrow with precision and care, infusing every shaft with the essence of his craftsmanship and wisdom.

Despite his advanced years, Hiroshi's passion for his craft burned as brightly as ever, and he continued to ply his trade with unwavering dedication and skill. Each day, he would rise with the sun, tending to his workshop with meticulous care, selecting the finest materials and honing his craft with each stroke of his hand.

One day, as Hiroshi worked diligently in his workshop, a weary traveler stumbled upon his doorstep, his face drawn and haggard from the trials of the road. Recognizing the traveler's need for shelter and sustenance, Hiroshi welcomed him into his home with open arms, offering food, drink, and a warm place by the fire.

As the traveler rested and recuperated, Hiroshi regaled him with tales of his life as an arrow maker—the joys and struggles, the triumphs and tribulations. He spoke of the artistry and precision required to craft each arrow, and the deep sense of fulfillment that came from seeing his creations take flight.

Inspired by Hiroshi's passion and wisdom, the traveler listened intently, hanging on his every word. And as the night wore on and the fire crackled merrily in the hearth, a bond of friendship and respect blossomed between them, forged in the shared warmth of the fire and the shared wisdom of their hearts.

In the days that followed, the traveler became a frequent visitor to Hiroshi's workshop, eager to learn the secrets of arrow making from the master craftsman himself. With patience and perseverance, Hiroshi took the traveler under his wing, teaching him the ancient techniques passed down through generations of arrow makers.

Under Hiroshi's guidance, the traveler's skills blossomed, and he soon became a skilled arrow maker in his own right. Together, they worked side by side in the workshop, sharing stories and laughter as they crafted arrows of exquisite beauty and precision.

And as the seasons turned and the years passed, the traveler came to understand that the true essence of arrow making lay not in the perfection of the craft itself, but in the connection forged between the arrow maker and his creations—the love and care poured into each shaft, and the spirit of the maker imbued in every arrow.

In Hiroshi's workshop, amidst the scent of wood and feathers, the traveler found not only a mentor and friend but a profound sense of purpose and belonging. And though his journey would eventually lead him far from the tranquil village and the wise old arrow maker, he carried with him the lessons learned and the memories shared, forever grateful for the gift of Hiroshi's guidance and friendship.

Reflection:

"The Arrow Maker" presents a profound meditation on craftsmanship, mentorship, and the enduring bonds of friendship.

Through the characters of Hiroshi and the traveler, we are drawn into a world where dedication to one's craft becomes a path to self-discovery and connection with others.

At its heart, the story celebrates the art of craftsmanship, embodied in Hiroshi's skillful hands and unwavering commitment to excellence. His workshop becomes a sanctuary of creativity and precision, where each arrow is meticulously crafted with love and care. Through his craft, Hiroshi imparts not only technical knowledge but also a deeper understanding of the value of dedication and passion in one's work.

Moreover, "The Arrow Maker" explores the transformative power of mentorship and guidance. Hiroshi's decision to take the traveler under his wing reflects a generosity of spirit and a recognition of the importance of passing on knowledge to the next generation. Through their shared experiences in the workshop, Hiroshi and the traveler form a bond that transcends mere teacher-student relationship, blossoming into a profound friendship based on mutual respect and admiration.

In contemplating this story, we are invited to reflect on the significance of pursuing excellence in our own lives, whatever form that may take. Whether through the pursuit of a creative passion or the dedication to mastering a skill, "The Arrow Maker" reminds us of the fulfillment that comes from pouring our hearts into our work and striving for excellence in all that we do.

The Jar of Honey

The sweetness of life's blessings and the appreciation of simple pleasures.

In a quaint village nestled amidst verdant meadows and swaying fields of wildflowers, there lived a humble beekeeper named Akio. Known throughout the land for his expertise in tending to bees and harvesting the finest honey, Akio took great pride in his craft, treating each hive with the utmost care and reverence.

One crisp autumn morning, as Akio tended to his hives, he noticed a peculiar sight—a small jar of honey tucked away in the corner of the apiary, its lid adorned with intricate patterns etched into the glass. Curious, Akio approached the jar and inspected it closely, marveling at its beauty and craftsmanship.

As he reached out to touch the jar, a voice echoed in his mind—a gentle whisper that seemed to emanate from the very essence of the honey itself. "Take heed, dear beekeeper," the voice murmured, "for within this jar lies a secret of great importance, waiting to be discovered by one with a pure heart and a thirst for knowledge."

Intrigued by the mysterious voice, Akio carefully uncorked the jar and dipped his finger into the golden liquid within, savoring the sweet taste of honey as it danced upon his tongue. With each drop, he felt a sense of clarity and understanding wash over him, as if the honey itself held the keys to unlocking the mysteries of the universe.

As the days turned into weeks and the weeks into months, Akio found himself drawn to the jar of honey time and time again, each encounter bringing him closer to unraveling its secrets. With each taste, he delved deeper into the hidden wisdom contained within, learning lessons of patience, gratitude, and the interconnectedness of all things.

Through the jar of honey, Akio discovered the beauty of simplicity and the importance of cherishing the small moments in life. He learned to appreciate the delicate dance of the bees as they flitted from flower to flower, gathering nectar to create the sweet elixir that brought joy to so many.

Moreover, Akio came to understand the power of intention and mindfulness in all that he did, recognizing that each action, no matter how small, held the potential to create profound ripples of impact in the world around him. With each jar of honey he harvested, he did so with a sense of reverence and gratitude, honoring the bees and the land that provided for him.

And as the seasons turned and the years passed, Akio's wisdom grew with each jar of honey he harvested, his heart overflowing with gratitude for the lessons learned and the beauty discovered along the way. In the jar of honey, he found not only a source of nourishment but a teacher and companion on the journey of life—a reminder of the sweetness that could be found in even the most unexpected of places.

Reflection:

"The Jar of Honey" offers a delightful allegory on the beauty of simplicity. Through the story of Akio and the mysterious jar of honey, we are invited to contemplate the profound lessons that can be found in the everyday moments of life.

The story speaks to the transformative power of mindfulness and intentionality in our actions. Akio's encounters with the jar of honey serve as a reminder of the importance of being present in the moment, and of approaching life with a sense of curiosity and wonder. Through his exploration of the honey's secrets, he learns to appreciate the beauty of the natural world and the interconnectedness of all things.

Moreover, "The Jar of Honey" highlights the value of gratitude and reverence in our interactions with the world around us. Akio's relationship with the bees and the land becomes one of reciprocity and respect, as he learns to cherish the gifts they provide and to approach his work with a sense of humility and gratitude.

In reflecting on this story, we are challenged to consider the ways in which we can cultivate mindfulness and gratitude in our own lives. Whether through the simple act of savoring a jar of honey or by taking time to appreciate the beauty of nature, we can find opportunities for growth and insight in the most unexpected of places.

Ultimately, "The Jar of Honey" encourages us to embrace the wisdom that can be found in simplicity. In a world filled with distractions and complexities, Akio's journey reminds us of the importance of slowing down, of finding joy in the small moments, and of seeking wisdom in the most unlikely of places.

The Wise Parrot

The wisdom found in unexpected places and the power of keen observation.

In the heart of a bustling marketplace, where merchants haggled over spices and fabrics, and the air was filled with the chatter of eager shoppers, there lived a wise parrot named Kavi. Perched atop a gilded cage in a small corner stall, Kavi watched the world with keen eyes, his vibrant feathers gleaming in the sunlight.

Kavi's life began many years ago in a distant forest, where he was born to a family of parrots known for their intelligence and wisdom. From a young age, Kavi showed a remarkable aptitude for learning, eagerly absorbing the lessons taught by his parents and elders.

As Kavi grew older, he ventured beyond the confines of the forest, embarking on a journey of discovery that would ultimately lead him to the bustling marketplace where he now resided. Along the way, he encountered a myriad of creatures, each with their own tales to tell and wisdom to impart.

It was during his travels that Kavi first learned of the human world—a world filled with wonders and mysteries that captivated his imagination. Drawn by the allure of the marketplace, Kavi decided to make it his home, eager to continue his quest for knowledge amidst the hustle and bustle of city life.

Day after day, as the marketplace bustled with activity, Kavi listened intently to the conversations of the merchants and the shoppers, soaking in the myriad tales and stories that filled the air. With each passing moment, he grew wiser still, his mind a treasure trove of knowledge and insight.

Despite his confinement within a gilded cage, Kavi's spirit remained unbroken. For he knew that true freedom came not from physical escape, but from the boundless expanse of the mind and the heart.

As dusk settled over the marketplace, casting long shadows across the cobblestone streets, a weary traveler stumbled upon Kavi's stall. Drawn by the brilliance of the wise parrot's plumage, the traveler approached with a sense of wonder and curiosity.

"Tell me, wise parrot," the traveler began, "what is the secret to happiness? How can one find peace in a world filled with chaos and uncertainty?"

Kavi regarded the traveler with a knowing gaze, his bright eyes shining with wisdom as he pondered the question. And then, with a gentle flutter of his wings, he spoke in a voice as soft as the breeze.

"The secret to happiness," Kavi said, "lies not in the pursuit of wealth or power, but in the simple pleasures of life—the warmth of the sun on your feathers, the melody of birdsong in the air, the love of friends and family gathered around you. True happiness comes from within, from embracing the beauty of the present moment and finding joy in the smallest of things."

The traveler listened intently to Kavi's words, his heart lightening with each passing moment. For in the wise parrot's simple wisdom, he found a sense of peace and clarity that had long eluded him.

And as the night deepened and the stars twinkled overhead, the traveler bid farewell to Kavi, his spirit uplifted by the encounter.

For in the wise parrot's words, he had found not only the secret to happiness but a renewed sense of purpose and hope.

And so, as the marketplace slumbered beneath the watchful gaze of the moon, Kavi sat perched in his gilded cage, his vibrant feathers glowing in the darkness. For though his wings may be clipped and his freedom restricted, the spirit of the wise parrot soared free, his voice a beacon of light and wisdom in a world filled with darkness.

Reflection:

"The Wise Parrot" offers a timeless lesson on the pursuit of happiness and the importance of finding joy in life's simple pleasures. Through the story of Kavi, we are reminded that true happiness comes not from external sources such as wealth or power, but from within—from embracing the beauty of the present moment and finding joy in the smallest of things.

Kavi's wisdom transcends the boundaries of his cage, offering a beacon of light and hope to all who encounter him. His message—that happiness is a choice, and that it can be found in even the most unlikely of places—resonates with timeless truth and beauty.

In reflecting on this story, we are challenged to consider the ways in which we can cultivate happiness and contentment in our own lives. Whether through the practice of mindfulness, the cultivation of gratitude, or the pursuit of meaningful connections with others, we can find opportunities for joy and fulfillment in every moment.

Ultimately, "The Wise Parrot" reminds us that happiness is not a destination to be reached, but a journey to be embraced. In the wise parrot's simple wisdom, we find a profound lesson on the importance of living mindfully, finding joy in the present moment, and embracing the beauty of life's journey.

The Woodcutter's Wealth

The rewards of hard work and the abundance found in gratitude.

In a small village nestled amidst towering trees and winding streams, there lived a woodcutter named Haru. Day after day, from dawn until dusk, Haru would venture into the forest, his axe slung over his shoulder and a song upon his lips, to earn his living by harvesting timber.

Despite his honest toil, Haru lived a modest existence, his days filled with hard work and little else. His small cottage was humble, his meals simple, and his pockets often empty. Yet, despite his lack of material wealth, Haru possessed a richness of spirit that shone brightly in the eyes of all who knew him.

One crisp autumn morning, as Haru set out into the forest to begin his day's work, he stumbled upon a hidden glade bathed in dappled sunlight. Intrigued by the sight, he ventured deeper into the glade, his curiosity piqued by the sense of tranquility that permeated the air.

To his astonishment, nestled amidst the golden leaves and moss-covered stones, Haru discovered a majestic tree unlike any he had ever seen before. Its trunk was sturdy and its branches stretched high into the sky, bearing fruit of the most vibrant hues.

In awe of the tree's beauty, Haru approached cautiously, his heart filled with wonder and reverence. And as he reached out to touch its bark, a voice echoed in his mind—a gentle whisper that seemed to emanate from the very essence of the tree itself.

"Take heed, dear woodcutter," the voice murmured, "for within this glade lies a treasure of great importance, waiting to be discovered by one with a pure heart and a thirst for knowledge."

Intrigued by the mysterious voice, Haru looked around the glade, his eyes scanning the ground for any sign of hidden treasure. Yet, try as he might, he could find nothing of value amidst the fallen leaves and tangled underbrush.

Frustrated and disheartened, Haru sank to his knees, his mind awash with disappointment. For despite his efforts, he could not fathom where the treasure might be hidden or what form it might take.

And then, as he sat in the quiet stillness of the glade, a realization dawned upon him—a realization that would change the course of his life forever.

For in that moment, Haru understood that true wealth could not be measured in gold or silver, but in the richness of the world around him—the beauty of the forest, the laughter of friends, and the love of family.

With a newfound sense of gratitude and appreciation, Haru returned to his cottage, his heart light and his spirit renewed. And though he may never uncover the treasure hidden within the glade, he knew that he was already richer than he had ever dared to imagine.

From that day forward, Haru lived his life with a sense of joy and contentment that filled every corner of his being. And though he continued to toil in the forest, his days were no longer spent in pursuit of wealth, but in celebration of the abundance that surrounded him.

For in the eyes of the wise woodcutter, true wealth lay not in the accumulation of riches, but in the simple pleasures of life and the beauty of the natural world—a treasure far more precious than any gold or silver could ever be.

Reflection:

"The Woodcutter's Wealth" invites us to reflect on the nature of true abundance and the richness of a life well-lived. Through the story of Haru, we are reminded that wealth is not merely measured in material possessions, but in the depth of our connections, the beauty of our surroundings, and the contentment that comes from within.

In contemplating this story, we are challenged to consider our own definitions of wealth and abundance. Are we too focused on acquiring material possessions, or do we recognize the true treasures that surround us each day—the laughter of loved ones, the beauty of nature, and the moments of quiet contentment that fill our lives?

Ultimately, "The Woodcutter's Wealth" challenges us to reevaluate our priorities and seek out the true treasures that enrich our lives—the beauty of nature, the warmth of human connection, and the contentment that comes from living with gratitude and mindfulness. In doing so, we can uncover a wealth far greater than anything money can buy—a wealth that resides in the depths of our hearts and souls and that exists within and around us.

The Lotus Flower

Purity and enlightenment, rising above adversity to bloom in beauty.

In the heart of a tranquil pond, amidst a sea of lily pads and emerald green foliage, there bloomed a single lotus flower of exquisite beauty. Its petals were a delicate shade of pink, tinged with hints of gold and lavender, and its fragrance filled the air with a sweet, intoxicating perfume.

For generations, the lotus flower had been revered by the villagers as a symbol of purity, enlightenment, and spiritual awakening. They believed that its blossoms held the key to unlocking the secrets of the universe and transcending the bonds of earthly existence.

And so, each day, the villagers would gather by the pond to pay homage to the lotus flower, offering prayers and incense in its honor. They believed that by communing with the sacred flower, they could attain enlightenment and find inner peace amidst the chaos of the world.

But as they bowed their heads in reverence, they failed to see the true beauty of the lotus flower—the beauty that lay not in its petals or fragrance, but in the simple act of being.

For the lotus flower did not strive to be beautiful or to inspire awe in those who beheld it. It simply existed, rooted firmly in the mud at the bottom of the pond, its petals unfolding gracefully in the gentle embrace of the sun.

And in its quiet strength and resilience, the lotus flower taught the villagers a powerful lesson about the nature of beauty and the essence of existence. For true beauty, it whispered, could not be found in external adornments or fleeting pleasures, but in the purity of the soul and the depth of the heart.

As the villagers gazed upon the lotus flower, they felt a sense of peace and tranquility wash over them, their hearts filled with a profound sense of gratitude and reverence. And in that moment, they understood that true enlightenment could only be found in the stillness of the heart and the depths of the soul, where the lotus flower bloomed eternal and unchanging, a symbol of hope and beauty in a world filled with chaos and uncertainty.

But as time passed and the seasons changed, the villagers began to take the lotus flower for granted, their daily rituals becoming mere routines devoid of meaning or significance. They bowed their heads in empty gestures, their minds consumed by worries and distractions, and they failed to see the beauty that lay right before their eyes.

And so, the lotus flower withered and faded, its once vibrant petals turning brown and brittle as the life slowly drained from its veins. The villagers watched in dismay as their beloved symbol of enlightenment and beauty succumbed to the ravages of time, their hearts heavy with regret and sorrow.

But amidst the despair and desolation, a single bud emerged from the murky depths of the pond, its delicate petals unfurling to reveal a new lotus flower of even greater beauty and splendor than before.

And as the villagers gathered by the pond to witness the miracle of rebirth, they realized that true beauty could never truly be lost or destroyed—it could only be transformed and renewed, like the lotus flower that bloomed eternal in the depths of their souls.

And so, with hearts full of gratitude and reverence, the villagers once again bowed their heads in homage to the lotus flower, their spirits lifted by the promise of new beginnings and the timeless beauty of the natural world. And as they gazed upon the flower in awe and wonder, they understood that true enlightenment could only be found in the simplicity of the present moment and the eternal cycle of life and death that bound them all together.

Reflection:

"The Lotus Flower" offers a profound reflection on the nature of beauty, enlightenment, and the essence of existence. Through the imagery of the lotus flower, the story invites us to contemplate the deeper truths of life and the timeless wisdom inherent in the natural world.

At its core, the lotus flower symbolizes purity, resilience, and spiritual awakening. Its ability to bloom amidst the murky depths of the pond, untouched by the impurities that surround it, serves as a powerful metaphor for the human journey towards enlightenment and self-realization.

Moreover, "The Lotus Flower" challenges us to reevaluate our perceptions of enlightenment and spiritual awakening. While the villagers in the story initially seek enlightenment through external rituals and practices, they ultimately discover that true enlightenment can only be found in the stillness of the heart and the depths of the soul.

As we reflect on this story, we are encouraged to be reminded of the interconnectedness of all things and the eternal cycle of life and death that binds us together. Just as the lotus flower blooms eternal amidst the changing seasons, so too do we find renewal and rebirth in the ever-unfolding journey of existence.

The Precious Gem

The value of inner richness over external wealth.

In the bustling city of Mathura, renowned for its vibrant markets and skilled artisans, there lived a young merchant named Rajiv. Despite his humble beginnings, Rajiv possessed a keen eye for beauty and a shrewd business sense that had earned him a reputation as one of the most successful traders in the region.

One day, as Rajiv perused the market stalls in search of rare treasures to add to his collection, his gaze fell upon a small, unassuming gemstone nestled amidst a pile of glittering jewels. Intrigued by its simple elegance and radiant glow, Rajiv approached the merchant with a curious heart.

"What is the story behind this gemstone?" Rajiv inquired, his eyes sparkling with fascination.

The merchant regarded Rajiv with a knowing smile, his weathered face lined with the wisdom of years. "Ah, this is no ordinary gemstone," he replied. "Legend has it that this precious gem holds the power to grant its owner three wishes—three wishes that can change the course of destiny itself."

Intrigued by the merchant's words, Rajiv eagerly purchased the gemstone and hurried home to ponder the possibilities that lay before him. As he held the gemstone in his hands, he felt a surge of excitement and anticipation coursing through his veins, his mind awash with dreams of wealth, power, and fame.

But as the days turned into weeks and the weeks into months, Rajiv found himself paralyzed by indecision, unsure of how best to use the power of the precious gem. Each night, he would lie awake in bed, wrestling with conflicting desires and fears of the unknown, unable to take action for fear of making the wrong choice.

And so, the gemstone lay forgotten on Rajiv's bedside table, its radiant glow dimmed by the weight of his indecision and doubt. But unbeknownst to Rajiv, the true power of the gemstone lay not in the granting of wishes, but in the journey of self-discovery and growth that it inspired.

One night, as Rajiv tossed and turned in his sleep, he was visited by a vivid dream—a dream in which he saw himself standing at the crossroads of destiny, faced with a choice that would shape the course of his life forever.

In the dream, Rajiv saw himself standing before a vast expanse of wilderness, with no clear path to guide him on his journey. And as he gazed out into the unknown, he felt a sense of fear and uncertainty wash over him, threatening to consume him whole.

But then, as if by magic, the precious gemstone appeared before him, glowing with an inner light that illuminated the darkness and banished his fears. And in that moment, Rajiv realized that the true power of the gemstone lay not in the granting of wishes, but in the courage and determination that it inspired within him.

With newfound resolve, Rajiv awoke from his dream with a sense of clarity and purpose that he had never known before. He knew now that he did not need the power of the gemstone to achieve his dreams, for the true power lay within himself—all he needed was the courage to take the first step on his journey.

And so, with a heart full of hope and determination, Rajiv set out into the world once more, ready to face whatever challenges lay ahead with courage and grace. And though he may never have used the power of the precious gem to grant his wishes, he knew that he had already received the greatest gift of all—the gift of self-discovery and the courage to chase his dreams, no matter where they may lead.

Reflection:

"The Precious Gem" serves as a powerful allegory for the journey of self-discovery and the true nature of fulfillment. Through Rajiv's quest to unlock the potential of the gemstone, we are reminded of the inherent human desire for wealth, power, and external validation. However, as Rajiv grapples with the weight of his indecision and the fear of making the wrong choice, we witness the limitations of material possessions in bringing lasting happiness.

The gemstone, with its promise of granting three wishes, symbolizes the allure of external solutions to life's challenges. Yet, as Rajiv discovers, true fulfillment cannot be found in external riches alone. Instead, it is the journey of self-discovery, courage, and personal growth that leads to genuine happiness and fulfillment.

Through his dream, Rajiv realizes that the true power lies within himself—the power to overcome obstacles, face fears, and pursue his dreams with unwavering determination. The gemstone serves as a catalyst for his inner transformation, guiding him to recognize his own strength and resilience.

Ultimately, "The Precious Gem" reminds us that happiness is not found in the pursuit of external rewards, but in the courage to follow our hearts and pursue our passions with authenticity and purpose. It encourages us to look within ourselves for the answers we seek and to embrace the journey of self-discovery as the true source of fulfillment in life.

The Two Acrobats

The balance between risk and trust in the pursuit of harmony.

In the heart of a bustling metropolis, where the streets pulsed with the rhythm of life and the air hummed with the chatter of bustling crowds, there resided two extraordinary acrobats named Ravi and Maya. Their names echoed through the city like whispers of magic, for they were renowned far and wide for their awe-inspiring displays of agility and grace that left audiences spellbound and breathless.

Ravi, with his keen eye for detail, could effortlessly gauge distances and angles with his one good eye, compensating for his lack of depth perception with sheer instinct and intuition. Maya, despite the stiffness in her crippled leg, possessed a strength and flexibility that belied her physical limitations, her every movement a testament to the power of perseverance and determination.

Despite their outward success, Ravi and Maya carried a burden hidden from the eyes of their fans—a burden that threatened to cast a shadow over their illustrious careers. For Ravi, the twinkle in his eye masked the fact that he was blind in one eye, a silent obstacle that lurked beneath his confident exterior. And Maya, with her dazzling smile and nimble movements, concealed the truth of her crippled leg, a constant reminder of the challenges she faced with every leap and bound.

As they prepared for their latest performance in the sprawling city square, Ravi and Maya found themselves engulfed in a maelstrom of doubt and uncertainty. The weight of their disabilities bore down upon them like a heavy shroud, threatening to suffocate their dreams of success and tarnish the glittering facade of their reputation.

With each somersault and pirouette, they grappled with the fear that their limitations would betray them, robbing them of the flawless perfection that their audience had come to expect. They feared that their disabilities would render them unworthy of the adoration and admiration that had once been their lifeblood, leaving them stranded in a sea of doubt and despair.

But just as they were on the brink of despair, a wise old sage approached them with a twinkle in his eye and a knowing smile on his lips. "Fear not, my friends," he said, his voice gentle yet firm. "For true greatness lies not in the absence of limitations, but in the courage to overcome them."

With these words of wisdom ringing in their ears, Ravi and Maya took to the stage with renewed determination and resolve, their hearts ablaze with the fire of possibility. With every twist and turn, they defied the odds and silenced their inner demons, proving to themselves and the world that their disabilities were not barriers to be overcome, but challenges to be embraced and conquered.

As the crowd erupted into applause at the conclusion of their performance, Ravi and Maya shared a knowing glance, their hearts overflowing with gratitude and pride. For in that moment, they realized that their disabilities were not obstacles to be overcome, but badges of honor that testified to their resilience and strength of spirit.

And so, as they took their final bow and bid farewell to the cheering crowd, Ravi and Maya knew that they had achieved something far greater than mere success—they had discovered the true meaning of courage, perseverance, and the indomitable human spirit.

For in the end, it is not our limitations that define us, but our willingness to face them head-on and emerge victorious in the face of adversity. And as Ravi and Maya learned, true greatness lies not in the absence of challenges, but in the courage to rise above them and soar to new heights of achievement and fulfillment.

Reflection:

"The Two Acrobats" is a poignant tale that speaks to the resilience of the human spirit and the power of determination in the face of adversity. Through the characters of Ravi and Maya, we are reminded that limitations need not define us, but rather serve as opportunities for growth and self-discovery.

The story underscores the importance of courage and perseverance in overcoming obstacles and achieving one's dreams. Despite facing physical challenges, Ravi and Maya refuse to succumb to self-doubt and fear, choosing instead to embrace their vulnerabilities and showcase their talents to the world.

Their journey serves as a powerful reminder that true greatness lies not in the absence of limitations, but in the courage to confront them with grace and dignity. By transcending their disabilities and delivering a breathtaking performance, Ravi and Maya inspire others to believe in themselves and pursue their aspirations with unwavering determination.

Ultimately, "The Two Acrobats" encourages us to embrace our own challenges and setbacks as opportunities for growth and transformation. It reminds us that with resilience, perseverance, and a positive mindset, we can overcome any obstacle and achieve success beyond our wildest dreams.

The Peacock's Dance

The celebration of life and the expression of one's unique beauty.

In a lush forest grove, where sunlight filtered through the emerald canopy and the air was alive with the symphony of nature, there dwelled a magnificent peacock named Amar. With feathers of iridescent blue and green that shimmered like precious gems in the dappled light, Amar was the undisputed king of the forest, his beauty and grace unparalleled by any other creature in the land.

Each day, as the sun dipped below the horizon and the shadows lengthened across the forest floor, Amar would perform his mesmerizing dance—a spectacle of color and movement that enchanted all who beheld it. With each graceful step and elegant flourish, he wove a tapestry of magic and wonder that captivated the hearts of all who bore witness to his splendor.

Yet amidst the adoration and applause that greeted his every performance, Amar carried a secret sorrow—a sorrow that lay hidden beneath the facade of his dazzling plumage and regal bearing. For you see, Amar danced not out of joy or exuberance, but out of obligation and duty, his every movement a reflection of the expectations placed upon him by the forest's inhabitants.

For generations, the peacock had been revered as a symbol of beauty and majesty, his dance a sacred ritual that heralded the changing of the seasons and the cycles of nature. But as the weight of tradition bore down upon him, Amar found himself longing for something more—a chance to dance not out of obligation, but out of pure, unbridled joy.

One day, as he wandered through the forest in search of solace, Amar chanced upon a wise old owl perched atop a moss-covered branch, its piercing eyes gazing down upon him with a knowing glint. "Why so troubled, young one?" the owl inquired, its voice soft yet penetrating. "Surely a creature as magnificent as yourself should have no cause for sorrow."

With a heavy heart, Amar poured out his woes to the wise old owl, recounting the burden of expectation that weighed upon him and the longing in his soul for freedom and self-expression. To his surprise, the owl listened intently to his tale, nodding sagely as Amar spoke of his deepest desires and fears.

"My dear friend," the owl said, its voice gentle yet firm, "true beauty lies not in the performance of duty, but in the expression of the soul. If it is joy and freedom you seek, then dance not for the approval of others, but for the sheer delight of dancing itself."

Inspired by the owl's words of wisdom, Amar returned to the heart of the forest with a newfound sense of purpose and determination. With each graceful step and elegant leap, he cast aside the shackles of expectation and obligation, allowing his heart to soar free and unencumbered by the weight of tradition.

And as the moon rose high in the night sky and the stars twinkled overhead, Amar danced the dance of his dreams—a dance of joy and liberation that echoed through the forest like a melody of pure, unadulterated bliss. And in that moment, he knew that true beauty lay not in the perfection of form or technique, but in the authenticity of expression and the freedom to be oneself.

For Amar the peacock, the greatest dance of all was not the one performed for the eyes of others, but the one danced for the sheer joy of dancing itself—a dance that spoke to the deepest depths of his soul and set his spirit ablaze with the fire of passion and purpose.

Reflection:

In the enchanting tale of "The Peacock's Dance," we're given a poignant reminder of the complexities of external perception versus internal fulfillment. While Amar's dance dazzles and delights those around him, it conceals a deeper longing for authenticity and freedom. His struggle reflects the universal human experience of navigating societal pressures and personal desires, reminding us that true fulfillment often lies in aligning our actions with our innermost truths.

The wise counsel of the old owl offers a guiding light for Amar and for us all. By encouraging him to dance from the depths of his soul rather than for the approval of others, the owl imparts a timeless lesson on the importance of self-expression and authenticity. In a world that often values conformity over individuality, Amar's journey serves as a powerful reminder to honor our true selves and to find joy in the pursuit of our passions.

As we reflect on "The Peacock's Dance," let's ponder our own dances in life—those moments when we may feel compelled to perform for the expectations of others, and those moments when we dance freely, unbound by societal constraints. May we find inspiration in Amar's courage to follow his heart and in the wisdom of the owl's guidance, as we strive to live authentically and to embrace the beauty of our own unique dances.

The Tree of Life

The interconnectedness of all living beings and nurturing essence of nature.

In the heart of a lush forest, where sunlight filtered through the canopy of leaves and the air hummed with the song of birds, there stood a majestic tree known as the Tree of Life. Its towering branches reached toward the heavens, its roots delving deep into the rich soil of the earth, connecting the realms above and below in a sacred union of life and spirit.

For centuries, the Tree of Life had stood as a symbol of strength, resilience, and interconnectedness, its gnarled trunk bearing witness to the passage of time and the ebb and flow of the natural world. Its leaves whispered tales of ages past, while its roots drank deeply from the wellspring of wisdom that flowed beneath the surface of the earth.

To the creatures of the forest, the Tree of Life was more than just a mere tree—it was a beacon of hope, a source of nourishment, and a sanctuary of solace in times of need. From the smallest insect to the mightiest beast, all found shelter and sustenance beneath its sprawling branches, bound together in a web of interconnectedness that spanned the breadth of the forest.

But as the seasons changed and the years wore on, the Tree of Life began to show signs of distress. Its once vibrant leaves began to wither and fade, its branches drooping with the weight of age and weariness. And as the forest mourned the decline of its beloved guardian, whispers of fear and uncertainty rippled through the trees, casting a shadow over the land.

In the face of this looming crisis, the creatures of the forest banded together in a spirit of unity and solidarity, determined to save the Tree of Life from its impending demise. From the wise old owl to the playful squirrel, each contributed what they could, offering their wisdom, strength, and resources in service of a greater cause.

Through their collective efforts and unwavering determination, the forest denizens unearthed the root cause of the Tree of Life's decline—a dark and malevolent force that sought to drain its life force and extinguish its light forever. With courage and resolve, they confronted this shadowy menace, standing firm in defense of all that they held dear.

And as the battle raged on, a miracle unfolded before their eyes—the Tree of Life, imbued with the power of their collective love and devotion, began to bloom anew, its branches stretching toward the sky with renewed vigor and vitality. In its resplendent beauty, the forest found hope and renewal, a testament to the power of unity and the resilience of the human spirit.

As the sun dipped below the horizon and the stars twinkled overhead, the creatures of the forest gathered beneath the boughs of the Tree of Life, their hearts filled with gratitude and awe. For in that moment, they understood the true meaning of community, compassion, and the interconnectedness of all living things.

And as they basked in the warm glow of the moonlight, they knew that as long as the Tree of Life stood tall, their home would remain a sanctuary of life, love, and boundless possibility—a testament to the enduring power of nature and the indomitable spirit of those who call it home.

Reflection:

In the tale of "The Tree of Life," we are transported to a forest where the majestic Tree of Life stands as a symbol of strength, resilience, and interconnectedness. As the forest faces a crisis with the decline of this beloved guardian, the creatures band together in a remarkable display of unity and determination.

This story serves as a reminder of the power of community and collective action in the face of adversity. Just as the forest denizens rally together to save the Tree of Life, we are reminded of the strength that lies in solidarity and cooperation. In times of hardship, it is often through coming together, pooling our resources, and supporting one another that we find the resilience to overcome even the greatest of challenges.

The renewal of the Tree of Life, sparked by the collective love and devotion of the forest creatures, serves as a powerful metaphor for hope and regeneration. It reminds us that even in our darkest moments, there is always the potential for growth and renewal, and that by standing together, we can weather any storm and emerge stronger on the other side.

As we reflect on "The Tree of Life," let us consider the interconnectedness of all living things and the profound impact that our actions can have on the world around us. May we be inspired by the unity and resilience of the forest creatures, and strive to cultivate a sense of community and compassion for in doing so, we contribute to the ongoing renewal and regeneration of the world, ensuring that the spirit of the Tree of Life lives on in all of us.

The Two Frogs

The importance of courage and perseverance in the face of adversity.

In the heart of a lush, verdant forest, there lay a tranquil pond, its surface shimmering under the dappled sunlight that filtered through the canopy above. In this idyllic setting dwelled two frogs named Hopper and Lily, whose friendship blossomed amidst the lily pads and reeds that adorned their watery home.

Hopper was a lively and adventurous frog, his vibrant green skin speckled with patches of gold. He possessed boundless energy and an insatiable curiosity, always eager to explore the nooks and crannies of their pond and beyond. Lily, on the other hand, was a gentle and nurturing soul, her soft pink skin adorned with delicate patterns of lilac. She took great pleasure in tending to the flowers that grew along the water's edge, their colorful blooms a testament to her care and devotion.

Despite their differences, Hopper and Lily shared a deep bond forged by their shared experiences and mutual respect. Together, they embarked on countless adventures, leaping from lily pad to lily pad with grace and agility, their laughter echoing through the forest like the gentle melody of a babbling brook.

But one fateful day, as they frolicked in the shallows of their beloved pond, the tranquility of their surroundings was shattered by the sudden onset of a violent storm. Dark clouds gathered overhead, casting a shadow over the forest, and the air grew heavy with the promise of rain.

Alarmed by the approaching storm, Hopper and Lily sought refuge beneath the shelter of a nearby tree, their hearts pounding with fear and uncertainty. As the first drops of rain began to fall, they huddled together for warmth and comfort, their eyes wide with apprehension.

But as the storm intensified and the winds howled through the trees, it became clear that their makeshift shelter would not be enough to protect them from harm. With a sense of growing dread, Hopper and Lily watched as the waters of their pond swelled and surged, threatening to engulf them in its fury.

In a desperate bid for safety, Hopper and Lily clung to each other as they were swept away by the raging currents, their cries for help lost amidst the roar of the tempest. For hours, they struggled against the relentless onslaught of the storm, their strength waning with each passing moment.

Just when all hope seemed lost, a glimmer of light appeared on the horizon—a fallen branch floating nearby, its sturdy limbs offering a lifeline amidst the chaos. With renewed determination, Hopper and Lily seized hold of the branch, their weary bodies clinging desperately to its rough bark as it bobbed and swayed in the churning waters.

As the storm raged on around them, they clung to each other with a steadfast resolve, drawing strength from their unbreakable bond of friendship. And as dawn broke and the storm began to recede, Hopper and Lily found themselves washed ashore on the banks of the pond, battered and bruised but alive.

As they lay exhausted upon the muddy ground, they knew that they owed their survival not just to luck or chance, but to the unwavering support and companionship of each other. In the aftermath of the storm, Hopper and Lily emerged not only as survivors, but as symbols of resilience and hope for all who dwelled in the pond.

Their harrowing ordeal served as a reminder of the fragility of life and the power of friendship to weather even the fiercest of storms. And as they looked out upon the tranquil waters of their pond, Hopper and Lily knew that no matter what challenges lay ahead, they would face them together, side by side, their bond unbreakable and their spirits undaunted by the trials of the world.

Reflection:

In the tale of "The Two Frogs," we are reminded of the enduring power of friendship and resilience in the face of adversity. Hopper and Lily, despite their differences, exemplify the strength that comes from standing by one another, especially during life's storms.

Their journey through the tempestuous waters of the storm reflects the challenges we all face in life, where unexpected trials can sweep us off our feet. However, it is during these moments that the support of a true friend can make all the difference, providing comfort, courage, and strength when we need it most.

Their story teaches us the importance of companionship and solidarity, showing that together, we can weather even the most formidable challenges.

Ultimately, "The Two Frogs" invites us to reflect on the significance of friendship, resilience, and mutual support in navigating life's turbulent waters. It encourages us to cherish the bonds we share with others and to draw strength from them during life's most challenging moments. Just as Hopper and Lily found solace in each other's company, may we too find comfort and courage in the presence of our loved ones, knowing that together, we can overcome any storm.

The Jewel in the Robe

The hidden wisdom within simplicity and the discovery of inner riches.

In a bustling city nestled amidst rolling hills and fertile valleys, there lived a humble tailor named Raj. Known far and wide for his exquisite craftsmanship and attention to detail, Raj was renowned as the finest tailor in the land, his garments coveted by royalty and commoners alike.

Despite his skill and reputation, Raj lived a modest life, content to ply his trade in his small workshop tucked away in a quiet corner of the city. Day after day, he would sit hunched over his sewing machine, his nimble fingers flying across the fabric as he worked tirelessly to bring his creations to life.

One day, as Raj was putting the finishing touches on a magnificent robe commissioned by the king himself, he noticed something glinting amidst the folds of the fabric. Curious, he reached inside and pulled out a small jewel, its facets sparkling in the sunlight like a thousand stars.

Astounded by his discovery, Raj marveled at the beauty of the jewel, its brilliance casting a radiant glow upon the room. But as he held it in his hand, a pang of doubt crept into his heart. Should he keep the jewel for himself, he wondered, or should he return it to the king as an act of honesty and integrity?

After much deliberation, Raj made his decision. With a resolve as firm as the stitches in his finest garments, he set out for the royal palace, the jewel clutched tightly in his hand. As he approached the palace gates, his heart pounded with nervous anticipation, unsure of how the king would react to his unexpected arrival.

But to Raj's surprise, the king greeted him with open arms, his face lighting up with delight at the sight of the humble tailor. "Raj, my dear friend," the king exclaimed, "what brings you to my palace today?"

With trembling hands, Raj presented the jewel to the king, his voice steady despite the tumult of emotions swirling within him. "Your Majesty," he said, "I found this jewel in the robe I was sewing for you. I believe it belongs to you, and I have come to return it."

The king's eyes widened in astonishment as he accepted the jewel from Raj's outstretched hand. "Raj, you have done a great service to me and to our kingdom," he declared, his voice ringing with sincerity. "Your honesty and integrity are truly commendable, and I am grateful for your selfless act."

As a token of his appreciation, the king bestowed upon Raj a bag of gold coins, a reward for his honesty and integrity. But more valuable than any treasure was the king's trust and respect, a gift that Raj cherished above all else.

From that day forward, Raj's reputation as an honest and trustworthy tailor spread far and wide, his name spoken with reverence and admiration throughout the land. And as he continued to ply his trade in his small workshop, he did so with a heart full of pride and a spirit imbued with integrity, knowing that true wealth lies not in material possessions, but in the richness of one's character.

Reflection:

In "The Jewel in the Robe," Raj's story serves as a reminder of the importance of honesty, integrity, and the inherent value of doing what is right, even when faced with difficult choices.

Raj's decision to return the jewel to the king, despite the temptation to keep it for himself, highlights the power of integrity and the moral compass that guides us in times of uncertainty. His actions exemplify the timeless principle that honesty is not merely a virtue but a foundation upon which trust and respect are built.

Moreover, Raj's selflessness in returning the jewel underscore the notion that true wealth is not measured by material possessions but by the richness of one's character. By prioritizing integrity over personal gain, Raj demonstrates that integrity is the ultimate currency, enriching both the individual and the community at large.

"The Jewel in the Robe" prompts us to reflect on our own values and the choices we make in our daily lives. It challenges us to consider the importance of integrity in our interactions with others and the impact that our actions can have on those around us.

Ultimately, Raj's story inspires us to strive for integrity in all aspects of our lives, recognizing that true greatness lies not in the accumulation of wealth or status, but in the steadfast adherence to principles of honesty, integrity, and moral courage, which define who we truly are.

The Empty Boat

The freedom found in letting go and surrendering to the flow of life.

In the heart of a serene lake, nestled amidst a tranquil landscape of rolling hills and verdant forests, there floated an empty boat, its weathered wooden frame glistening in the golden light of the setting sun. The surface of the lake shimmered with a gentle radiance, mirroring the colors of the sky as they painted the horizon with hues of orange, pink, and purple.

The boat, though devoid of any occupants, seemed to possess a quiet allure, beckoning to those who chanced upon its tranquil sanctuary. Its oars lay still against the sides, the water lapping softly against its hull as it drifted aimlessly on the rippling surface. To some, it appeared as nothing more than an abandoned vessel adrift on the water, its purpose and origin shrouded in mystery. But to those who were attuned to its silent wisdom, the empty boat held a profound lesson, a timeless truth that transcended the boundaries of time and space.

One day, a weary traveler came upon the lake, his footsteps heavy with the weight of his burdens and the trials of his journey. As he gazed out upon the tranquil waters, his eyes were drawn to the empty boat floating serenely on the surface, its presence a stark contrast to the chaos and turmoil that churned within his soul. Intrigued by its silent invitation, the traveler approached the shore and called out to see if anyone was aboard, but there was no response. Undeterred, he waded into the water and climbed aboard the boat, his heart heavy with questions and doubts.

As he sat in the boat, his thoughts swirling like the waters beneath him, the traveler found himself overcome with a sense of peace and serenity unlike anything he had ever known. The stillness of the lake enveloped him like a warm embrace, and for the first time in a long while, he felt completely at ease. In that moment of quiet reflection, the traveler realized the profound lesson that the empty boat had to teach him.

Just as the boat floated effortlessly on the surface of the water, so too could he learn to let go of the burdens and worries that weighed him down and simply allow himself to be carried along by the currents of life. With each gentle sway of the boat, he felt the knots of tension in his shoulders begin to loosen, the worries that had plagued his mind slowly melting away like dew beneath the morning sun. In the embrace of the empty boat, the traveler found solace, clarity, and a renewed sense of purpose.

As the sun dipped below the horizon and the stars began to twinkle in the night sky, the traveler remained in the boat, his heart filled with gratitude for the peace and tranquility it had bestowed upon him. Though he could not say for certain who the boat belonged to or where it came from, he knew that its message would stay with him forever, a guiding light in the darkness, a beacon of hope and renewal in the vast expanse of the unknown.

For the empty boat was not just a vessel adrift on the water, but a symbol of the boundless potential that lies within each of us to find peace, contentment, and fulfillment in the midst of life's uncertainties. And as the traveler ventured forth into the unknown, he carried with him the silent wisdom of the empty boat, guiding him on his path and illuminating the way forward with its timeless message of acceptance, surrender, and inner peace.

Reflection:

"The Empty Boat" offers a profound reflection on the nature of inner peace and serenity amidst life's uncertainties. Through the symbolism of the empty boat drifting on the tranquil lake, the story invites us to contemplate the power of surrender, acceptance, and finding tranquility in the present moment.

The image of the empty boat serves as a metaphor for the human experience, with its calm presence amidst the ever-changing currents of life mirroring the potential for inner stillness and tranquility within each of us. Like the traveler who encounters the empty boat, we are often weighed down by the burdens and worries of the world, navigating the tumultuous waters of existence in search of solace and meaning.

Yet, as the traveler discovers, true peace is not found in the external circumstances of our lives, but in the willingness to let go of control and surrender to the flow of life's currents. In the quiet solitude of the empty boat, he finds a refuge from the noise and chaos of the world, allowing himself to be carried along by the gentle rhythm of the water.

The reflection prompts us to consider our own relationship with inner peace and tranquility. Are we able to find moments of stillness and serenity amidst the busyness of our lives? Do we struggle against the current, or do we surrender to the flow of life with trust and acceptance?

"The Empty Boat" encourages us to recognize that peace is not something we must seek outside of ourselves, but a state of being that resides within us, waiting to be discovered. Like the traveler who finds solace in the emptiness of the boat, we too can cultivate a sense of inner peace by letting go of attachments and expectations, and embracing the present moment with open hearts and minds.

Ultimately, the reflection invites us to consider the possibility of finding peace in the midst of life's uncertainties, and to embrace the wisdom of surrender as a pathway to inner fulfillment and contentment. Just as the empty boat drifts effortlessly on the tranquil waters of the lake, may we too learn to surrender to the flow of life, trusting in the journey and finding peace in the emptiness of the present moment.

The Seven Blows

The transformative power of adversity and the lessons learned through trials.

Deep in the heart of a secluded mountain valley, where the air was crisp and the sound of rushing water echoed off the towering cliffs, there lived a solitary monk named Siddharth. Renouncing the comforts of the world, Siddharth had devoted his life to the pursuit of enlightenment, seeking to unlock the mysteries of existence and find inner peace amidst the chaos of the world.

One day, as Siddharth meditated beneath the shade of a gnarled old tree, he was visited by a weary traveler who spoke of a legendary master who dwelled high atop the peaks of the distant mountains. It was said that this master possessed the power to grant enlightenment to those who proved themselves worthy, but that the path to his abode was fraught with peril and uncertainty.

Intrigued by the traveler's words, Siddharth resolved to seek out the master and learn from his wisdom, embarking on a journey that would test his resolve and challenge his understanding of the world. For seven long days and nights, Siddharth traversed treacherous terrain and weathered fierce storms, his determination unwavering as he pressed ever onward towards his goal.

At long last, Siddharth reached the summit of the highest peak, where he was greeted by the sight of a humble dwelling nestled amidst the clouds. Knocking gently on the door, he was welcomed inside by the master, who regarded him with a wise and knowing smile.

For seven days and seven nights, Siddharth sat at the master's feet, absorbing his teachings and pondering the mysteries of the universe. Each day, the master imparted upon him a new lesson -compassion, presence and mindfulness, impermanence, detachment, surrender and unity-, guiding him on the path to enlightenment and challenging him to transcend the limitations of his own mind.

But on the seventh day, as Siddharth prepared to depart, the master struck him with a blow that sent him reeling to the ground, his body wracked with pain and confusion. And with each subsequent blow, Siddharth felt his ego dissolve and his sense of self vanish into the ether, leaving him empty and vulnerable before the vastness of the cosmos.

In that moment of surrender, Siddharth experienced a profound revelation—a glimpse of the true nature of reality and the interconnectedness of all things. And as he lay upon the ground, battered and bruised, he realized that enlightenment could not be attained through the pursuit of knowledge or the accumulation of wisdom, but through the surrender of the self and the embrace of the present moment.

With a sense of clarity and purpose, Siddharth rose to his feet and bid farewell to the master, his heart filled with gratitude for the lessons he had learned and the journey that had brought him to this place. And as he descended from the mountain, he carried with him the knowledge that true enlightenment lay not in the attainment of perfection, but in the acceptance of imperfection and the willingness to embrace the journey, no matter where it may lead.

Reflection:

The tale of Siddharth's encounter with the master and the seven blows he received offers profound insights into the nature of enlightenment and the journey of self-discovery.

Each blow Siddharth receives symbolizes a fundamental aspect of the human experience and the obstacles we must overcome on the path to enlightenment. Through compassion, presence, impermanence, detachment, surrender, and unity, Siddharth learns valuable lessons about the nature of reality and the interconnectedness of all things.

The final blow, which leaves Siddharth battered and bruised, represents the ultimate surrender of the self and the ego. In that moment of vulnerability, Siddharth experiences a profound revelation about the true nature of existence and the interconnected web of life.

This reflection invites us to contemplate the nature of enlightenment and the journey of self-discovery. It reminds us that true wisdom cannot be attained through the accumulation of knowledge or the pursuit of perfection, but through the acceptance of imperfection and the willingness to surrender to the flow of life.

The Moon and the Empty Sky

The interconnectedness of all things and the vastness of the universe within.

In the tranquil stillness of a moonlit night, there existed a deep and profound connection between the moon and the empty sky. Each night, as the moon rose gracefully into the heavens, it cast its gentle glow upon the vast expanse of the sky, illuminating the darkness and bathing the world below in its ethereal light.

Yet, despite their intimate dance through the ages, the moon and the empty sky remained separate entities, each with its own distinct presence and essence. The moon, with its luminous beauty and serene radiance, held the gaze of all who beheld it, captivating hearts with its silent majesty. Its silvery beams danced across the landscape, painting the earth with soft hues of silver and gray, and casting enchanting shadows that danced upon the ground below. And the empty sky, vast and boundless, stretched endlessly in all directions, embracing the moon with open arms and cradling it in its infinite embrace, providing the canvas upon which its celestial dance unfolded.

As they moved in tandem across the celestial tapestry, the moon and the empty sky seemed to communicate in a language all their own—a language of silent understanding and profound wisdom. With each passing moment, they moved in perfect harmony, their movements synchronized in a delicate ballet of light and shadow. In their union, they embodied the timeless dance of creation and destruction, birth and death, light and darkness.

For the moon, with its waxing and waning phases, reflected the cyclical nature of existence, reminding all who gazed upon it of the impermanence of life and the eternal rhythm of the universe. Its phases mirrored the ebb and flow of time, marking the passage of days and seasons with quiet dignity and grace.

And the empty sky, with its boundless expansiveness, symbolized the limitless potential and infinite possibilities that lay within each moment. Within its depths, stars twinkled like diamonds in the night, casting their soft, silvery light upon the earth below and illuminating the darkness with their celestial glow.

Together, the moon and the empty sky wove a tapestry of beauty and wonder, inspiring awe and reverence in all who beheld their celestial dance. And as they journeyed through the night, they whispered secrets of the cosmos to those who dared to listen, imparting timeless wisdom and eternal truths to all who sought enlightenment.

Reflection:

The tale of "The Moon and the Empty Sky" invites us to contemplate the profound interconnectedness and beauty inherent in the natural world around us. Through the imagery of the moon and the empty sky, we are reminded of the timeless dance of existence, where each element plays a vital role in the grand symphony of the universe.

Just as the moon and the empty sky coexist in perfect harmony, so too are we interconnected with the world around us. The moon's radiant presence illuminates the darkness, symbolizing hope and guidance in times of uncertainty. Meanwhile, the empty sky represents boundless possibility and potential, reminding us of the infinite opportunities that await us in every moment.

As we reflect on the silent communion between the moon and the empty sky, we are encouraged to embrace the present moment and find solace in the simplicity of existence. Like the moon, we are reminded of the cyclical nature of life, where moments of light and darkness ebb and flow with the passage of time. And like the empty sky, we are urged to recognize the vast expanse of potential that lies within us, waiting to be explored and realized.

Ultimately, "The Moon and the Empty Sky" serves as a reminder of the interconnectedness of all things. Through its gentle imagery and profound wisdom, we are encouraged to recognize that we are but fleeting shadows beneath the eternal gaze of the moon and the empty sky.

The Empty Mirror

The nature of self-reflection and the realization of emptiness as liberation.

In the heart of a remote mountain monastery, nestled among the towering peaks and enveloped by the tranquil embrace of nature, there resided a revered monk known throughout the land as Master Chen. With his serene demeanor and penetrating gaze, Master Chen was revered by all who knew him for his wisdom and insight into the mysteries of existence. His presence alone seemed to radiate an aura of tranquility and enlightenment, drawing seekers from far and wide to seek his guidance and wisdom.

One crisp autumn morning, as the leaves danced in the gentle breeze and the air was filled with the sweet fragrance of incense, Master Chen summoned his disciples to gather in the courtyard for a profound lesson. As they assembled before him, their faces alight with anticipation and reverence, Master Chen beckoned them to "This mirror," Master Chen began, his voice soft yet commanding, "is more than just a reflection of the physical world. It is a mirror of the soul, reflecting the deepest truths and innermost thoughts of those who gaze upon it."

With a sweep of his hand, Master Chen gestured for his disciples to approach the mirror one by one and gaze deeply into its polished surface. As each disciple peered into the mirror, they were met with their own reflection, their features illuminated by the soft glow of the morning sun.

But as they stared into the mirror, something strange began to happen. The images reflected back at them began to shift and change, morphing into scenes from their past, present, and even future. Memories long forgotten resurfaced, dreams yet to be realized unfolded before their eyes, and hidden desires stirred within their hearts.

For some, the experience was exhilarating—a glimpse into the boundless possibilities of existence and the infinite potential of the human spirit. For others, it was unsettling—a confrontation with the shadows that lurked within their souls and the fears that held them back from embracing their true selves.

But through it all, Master Chen watched with a knowing smile, his eyes alight with wisdom and compassion. For he understood that the mirror was not merely a tool for self-reflection, but a doorway to enlightenment—a means of transcending the illusions of the ego and awakening to the deeper truths that lay beyond.

And as the disciples continued to gaze into the mirror, they realized that true enlightenment could not be found in the external world, but in the stillness of the mind and the clarity of perception. For in the empty mirror of the soul, they saw not just their own reflections, but the boundless expanse of the universe reflected back at them—a reminder of their interconnectedness with all living beings and the eternal dance of existence.

With this profound realization, the disciples bowed deeply before Master Chen, their hearts filled with gratitude for the lessons he had imparted upon them. And as they departed from the courtyard, their minds abuzz with newfound insight, they carried with them the knowledge that the empty mirror of the soul held the key to unlocking the deepest mysteries of existence, if only they had the courage to look within.

Reflection:

The tale of "The Empty Mirror" invites us to contemplate the profound nature of self-reflection and inner inquiry. Through the imagery of the mirror, we are encouraged to explore the depths of our own consciousness and confront the truths that lie hidden within.

Just as the disciples in the story were confronted with their own reflections and the myriad scenes that unfolded within the mirror, we too are reminded of the complexity of our own inner landscapes. The mirror serves as a metaphor for the mind, reflecting not only our outward appearances but also the thoughts, emotions, and memories that shape our identities.

As we journey through life, it's easy to become caught up in the external world—its distractions, its demands, and its illusions. Yet, true wisdom and understanding can only be found by turning inward, by bravely confronting the truths that lie within us.

The empty mirror symbolizes the vast expanse of consciousness—a space that is both infinite and boundless. In its emptiness, we find not a void, but rather a canvas upon which the tapestry of existence is painted. It is a mirror that reflects not just our individual selves, but the interconnectedness of all things.

Through self-reflection and introspection, we can begin to unravel the layers of conditioning and perception that cloud our vision and obscure the truth of who we are. By gazing into the empty mirror of the soul, we come to recognize the impermanence of our ego identities and the eternal nature of our true essence.

Ultimately, "The Empty Mirror" serves as a gentle reminder that the path to enlightenment begins with the willingness to look within—to confront the shadows and embrace the light, to acknowledge our flaws and celebrate our strengths, and to recognize that the greatest journey of all is the journey of self-discovery.

The Bamboo Acrobat

The balance between strength and flexibility in the pursuit of harmony.

In a quaint village nestled amidst rolling hills and swaying bamboo groves, there lived a young acrobat named Kavi. With nimble limbs and a heart full of dreams, Kavi dazzled audiences with his breathtaking performances, captivating hearts with his graceful movements and daring feats.

But behind the facade of confidence and skill, Kavi harbored a secret fear—a fear of failure that gnawed at his spirit and threatened to shatter his dreams. For you see, Kavi was not like other acrobats. Though his body moved with precision and grace, his mind was plagued by doubt and uncertainty, his thoughts consumed by the fear of falling and the shame of disappointment.

One day, as Kavi prepared for his latest performance in the village square, he found himself paralyzed by fear, his limbs trembling and his heart pounding in his chest. Try as he might, he could not shake the feeling of dread that gripped him, nor could he silence the voice of self-doubt that whispered in his ear.

As the crowd gathered and the music began to play, Kavi forced himself to take the stage, his steps heavy and hesitant. With each leap and somersault, he felt the weight of his fear bearing down upon him, threatening to overwhelm his resolve and send him crashing to the ground below.

But just as he was on the brink of despair, a voice called out from the crowd—a voice filled with warmth and encouragement, belonging to an old bamboo farmer named Lao. "Fear not, young one," Lao said, his eyes twinkling with wisdom. "For the bamboo knows the secret of resilience, and it is a lesson that you too must learn."

With these words of wisdom ringing in his ears, Kavi closed his eyes and took a deep breath, summoning the courage to face his fears head-on. As he opened his eyes and looked out at the sea of expectant faces before him, he felt a newfound sense of determination welling up inside him, a determination to defy the odds and prove to himself and the world that he was capable of greatness.

With a renewed sense of purpose, Kavi launched into his routine, his movements fluid and effortless, his fear melting away with each twist and turn. As he soared through the air with the grace of a bird in flight, he felt a sense of liberation wash over him, a feeling of freedom that transcended the limitations of his own mind.

As the final notes of music faded into the air and Kavi landed gracefully on the ground, the crowd erupted into applause, their cheers echoing off the surrounding hills. But more importantly, Kavi felt a sense of pride and accomplishment swell within him, a recognition of his own inner strength and resilience.

From that day forth, Kavi no longer allowed fear to hold him back. With each performance, he embraced the lessons of the bamboo, drawing strength from its resilience and flexibility, and channeling that strength into his own artistry.

And as he danced beneath the moonlit sky, surrounded by the rustling bamboo and the gentle whispers of the wind, Kavi knew that he had found his true calling—a calling that would carry him to new heights of achievement and fulfillment, and inspire all who beheld his grace and courage.

Reflection:

The tale of "The Bamboo Acrobat" offers a reflection on overcoming fear and self-doubt to achieve one's full potential. It reminds us that courage is not the absence of fear, but the willingness to confront it head-on and push past our limitations.

In Kavi's journey, we see ourselves reflected—the moments of uncertainty, the nagging self-doubt, and the overwhelming fear of failure. Yet, through his perseverance and the guidance of the wise bamboo farmer, Kavi discovers the inner strength to rise above his fears and embrace his true potential.

This story prompts us to examine our own fears and insecurities, encouraging us to confront them with courage and determination. Like Kavi, we are reminded that true growth often lies on the other side of fear, and that by facing our challenges head-on, we can unlock new levels of strength and resilience.

The symbolism of the bamboo serves as a powerful metaphor for resilience and flexibility. Just as the bamboo bends but does not break in the face of adversity, so too can we learn to adapt and persevere in the midst of life's challenges.

Ultimately, "The Bamboo Acrobat" inspires us to embrace our fears, trust in our abilities, and take bold leaps toward our dreams. It reminds us that within each of us lies the power to overcome obstacles and achieve greatness, if only we have the courage to believe in ourselves.

The Empty Cup

The openness and receptivity for spiritual growth and enlightenment.

In a bustling city nestled between towering skyscrapers and bustling streets, there lived a humble tea master named Chen. Renowned throughout the land for his skillful hands and gentle demeanor, Chen ran a small tea shop tucked away in a quiet corner of the city, where he brewed the finest teas and welcomed weary travelers with open arms.

Despite his outward success, Chen harbored a secret sorrow that weighed heavily on his heart—a sorrow born from the loss of his beloved wife, Mei, who had passed away many years ago. Since her passing, Chen had struggled to find solace in his work, his once vibrant spirit dimmed by the ache of loneliness and longing.

One day, as Chen prepared for another day of business in his tea shop, he was visited by a mysterious traveler who entered the shop with a curious glint in his eye. Sensing the traveler's silent inquiry, Chen greeted him warmly and invited him to sit at the small wooden table in the center of the shop.

"Welcome, traveler," Chen said, pouring a cup of fragrant jasmine tea for his guest. "What brings you to my humble shop on this fine day?"

The traveler regarded Chen with a knowing smile, his eyes twinkling with wisdom. "I have come seeking the wisdom of a master," he said, his voice soft yet commanding. "I have heard tales of your skill and your kindness, and I wish to learn from you."

Intrigued by the traveler's request, Chen nodded thoughtfully and poured him a cup of tea. As the traveler sipped the tea, Chen watched him closely, his heart heavy with the weight of his own sorrow.

"You carry a heavy burden, my friend," the traveler said, setting down his cup with a gentle sigh. "But tell me, what is it that weighs so heavily on your heart?"

Moved by the traveler's compassion, Chen hesitated for a moment before sharing his tale of love and loss, of joy and sorrow. He spoke of his beloved wife, Mei, and the emptiness that had consumed him since her passing, leaving him adrift in a sea of grief and despair.

The traveler listened intently to Chen's story, his eyes filled with understanding. And when Chen had finished, the traveler reached out and touched his hand, his touch gentle yet reassuring.

"Your cup is empty, my friend," the traveler said, his voice filled with compassion. "But it is not your sorrow that fills it—it is your love. For in the emptiness of your grief lies the fullness of your heart, a heart that beats with the rhythm of love and longing."

With these words, the traveler rose from his seat and bowed respectfully to Chen, his eyes alight with wisdom. And as he made his way to the door, he turned back to Chen one final time, his smile radiant with hope.

"Remember, my friend," the traveler said, his voice echoing through the quiet space of the tea shop. "In the emptiness of the cup lies the promise of renewal, of new beginnings and endless possibilities.

Embrace the emptiness, and you will find the fullness of life waiting to be discovered."

And with that, the traveler disappeared into the bustling streets of the city, leaving Chen alone with his thoughts and his tea. And as he gazed upon the empty cup before him, Chen felt a sense of peace wash over him, his heart filled with the promise of a new day dawning.

Reflection:

In the story of "The Empty Cup," we are reminded of the profound wisdom that can be found in moments of emptiness and stillness. Chen, the humble tea master, carries within him a heavy burden of grief and longing following the loss of his beloved wife. His heartache fills him with a sense of emptiness, yet it is this very emptiness that becomes the vessel for transformation and renewal.

The arrival of the mysterious traveler serves as a catalyst for Chen's journey towards healing and self-discovery. Through their exchange, Chen is gently guided to recognize that the emptiness he feels is not solely a void of sorrow, but also a space where love and memories reside. This realization reframes Chen's perception of his grief, transforming it from a burden to a source of strength and connection.

The metaphor of the empty cup becomes a powerful symbol in the story, representing both Chen's sorrow and the potential for renewal. It serves as a reminder that within every emptiness lies the possibility for something new to emerge, whether it be healing, growth, or profound insight. Just as a cup must be emptied before it can be filled anew, so too must Chen embrace his emptiness before he can find solace and renewal.

Ultimately, "The Empty Cup" invites us to embrace the inherent emptiness of life with an open heart and mind. It encourages us to see beyond the surface of our sorrows and challenges, recognizing that within every moment of emptiness lies the opportunity for growth and transformation. Like Chen, we are reminded to trust in the process of life, knowing that even in our darkest moments, there is always the potential for light to shine through.

The Old Ox

The wisdom found in simplicity and the strength derived from inner peace.

In the serene countryside, where verdant pastures stretched out beneath the open sky and the air was sweet with the scent of wildflowers, there dwelled an old ox named Bao. Once a stalwart companion to the farmers who tilled the land, Bao had spent many years laboring in the fields, his powerful muscles plowing the earth and his steady gait pulling carts laden with grain and produce. But now, in the twilight of his life, Bao had been granted the gift of retirement, a respite from the rigors of work that allowed him to spend his days in quiet contemplation and leisurely grazing.

Despite the weariness that crept into his bones and the aches that lingered in his joints, Bao possessed a serene wisdom that came only with age and experience. He had witnessed the passing of countless seasons, each one bringing its own joys and sorrows, its own triumphs and trials. And through it all, Bao had remained a steadfast observer of life, attuned to the subtle rhythms of the natural world and the ebb and flow of existence.

One warm afternoon, as Bao lounged beneath the shade of a majestic oak tree, he was joined by a young calf named Mei. Eager and spirited, Mei had only recently joined the herd, her days filled with boundless energy and insatiable curiosity. She regarded Bao with wide, curious eyes, her tail swishing eagerly as she approached.

"Old Bao," Mei exclaimed, her voice tinged with awe, "how is it that you seem so content, even in your old age? What is the secret to a long and happy life?"

Bao regarded Mei with a gentle smile, his weathered face crinkling with the weight of years gone by. "Ah, little one," he replied, his voice a deep rumble like distant thunder, "the secret to a fulfilling life lies not in the pursuit of grandeur or glory, but in the simple pleasures that surround us each and every day."

With that, Bao rose to his feet, the earth trembling slightly beneath his massive frame. "Come," he said, nodding toward the sun-drenched meadow that stretched out before them, "let me show you the beauty of the world."

And so, side by side, Bao and Mei embarked on a leisurely stroll through the sun-kissed fields, their hooves sinking into the soft, fragrant earth with each step. They paused to nibble on tender grasses and drink from cool, babbling streams, their hearts filled with a sense of peace and contentment.

As they wandered, Bao shared tales of his youth—the adventures he had embarked upon, the challenges he had overcome, and the lessons he had learned along the way. He spoke of the changing seasons and the cyclical nature of life, of the importance of patience, resilience, and perseverance in the face of adversity.

And as the day stretched into evening and the sky blazed with the fiery hues of sunset, Bao and Mei found themselves bathed in the warm glow of twilight, their spirits lifted by the beauty of the world around them. In that moment, they understood that true happiness could be found not in the pursuit of wealth or status, but in the simple act of being alive, of savoring each precious moment and cherishing the gifts that life bestowed upon them.

For in the heart of the countryside, amidst the gentle rustle of leaves and the chorus of crickets, Bao and Mei had discovered the true secret to a long and happy life: to live each day with gratitude and grace, and to find joy in the journey, no matter where it may lead.

Reflection:

In the story of "The Old Ox," we are invited to contemplate the wisdom that comes with age and the simple joys of life that often go unnoticed in our pursuit of grander ambitions. Through the character of Bao, the old ox, we are reminded of the value of slowing down, appreciating the beauty of nature, and finding contentment in the present moment.

Bao's tranquil demeanor and profound insights serve as a powerful reminder that true happiness is not found in material wealth or worldly success, but in the connections we forge with others and the moments we share with the world around us. His willingness to impart his wisdom to the young calf, Mei, underscores the importance of passing down knowledge and nurturing the next generation with kindness and compassion.

As we reflect on Bao's story, we are encouraged to examine our own lives and consider the ways in which we can cultivate a deeper sense of gratitude and appreciation for the simple pleasures that surround us. Whether it be the warmth of the sun on our skin, the melody of birdsong in the air, or the company of loved ones by our side, there is beauty to be found in every moment if only we take the time to pause and truly experience it.

Ultimately, "The Old Ox" reminds us that life is a journey to be savored, filled with moments of joy, sorrow, and everything in between. By embracing each experience with an open heart and a spirit of curiosity, we can find fulfillment and meaning in even the most ordinary of moments, and discover a profound sense of peace and contentment in the process.

The Lost Horse

Serendipity in misfortune, revealing life's unpredictable blessings.

In a serene village nestled among emerald hills and verdant valleys, there dwelled a diligent farmer named Chen. His days were spent toiling under the sun's warm embrace, cultivating the fertile land that sustained both him and his family. Chen was a man of simple pleasures, finding joy in the gentle sway of the crops and the symphony of nature that surrounded him.

One fateful morning, as Chen tended to his fields with care, a magnificent stallion galloped past, its coat gleaming in the golden light of dawn. Chen watched in awe as the majestic creature raced across the horizon, its hooves pounding against the earth like thunder. Mesmerized by the sight, he couldn't help but marvel at the beauty and power of the wild horse.

Days turned into weeks, and still, there was no sign of the stallion's return. Chen searched the vast countryside, hoping against hope to catch a glimpse of the lost horse, but his efforts were in vain. As time passed, the memory of the magnificent creature began to fade, and Chen resigned himself to the possibility that it was gone forever.

But just when he had all but given up hope, fate intervened in the most unexpected way. One evening, as Chen returned home from a long day's work, he was greeted by a sight that took his breath away—the lost horse had returned, and it was not alone. Behind it trailed a herd of wild mustangs, their sleek bodies shimmering in the fading light of the setting sun.

Overwhelmed with joy and gratitude, Chen welcomed the horses into his care, knowing that they would bring prosperity and abundance to his family and the entire village. With each passing day, the herd grew larger and stronger, and Chen's fields flourished under their watchful gaze.

But just as things seemed to be looking up, tragedy struck. During a spirited ride on one of the wild stallions, Chen's son was thrown from the horse's back, landing with a sickening thud on the hard ground below. As Chen rushed to his son's side, fear and anguish gripped his heart, threatening to overwhelm him with despair.

But in the midst of his pain and sorrow, Chen remembered the timeless wisdom of the lost horse—a wisdom that had sustained him through the darkest of times. With a heavy heart and tear-filled eyes, he whispered the words to himself like a sacred mantra, finding solace in their profound truth.

"It is what it is," Chen murmured, his voice barely above a whisper. "Who is to say what is good or bad?"

In that moment of clarity, Chen understood that life was filled with both joy and sorrow, triumph and tragedy. And though he could not change the events that had transpired, he could choose how to respond to them—with courage, resilience, and an unwavering faith in the inherent goodness of the universe.

And so, as Chen tended to his son's broken body with tender care and loving kindness, he did so with a heart full of gratitude for the lessons he had learned and the wisdom he had gained. For in the end, it was not the events themselves that defined his life, but the way in which he chose to embrace them—with open arms and an unwavering spirit of resilience.

Reflection:

"The Lost Horse" offers a profound meditation on the nature of happiness and suffering, and the interconnectedness of joy and sorrow in the tapestry of life. Through Chen's journey, we are reminded of the impermanence of all things, and the futility of attaching ourselves to the fleeting highs and lows of existence.

In the face of adversity, Chen's response—"It is what it is, who is to say what is good or bad?"—serves as a powerful reminder of the importance of acceptance and equanimity in navigating life's ups and downs. Rather than clinging to our expectations and judgments, we are invited to embrace the present moment with open hearts and minds, knowing that every experience, whether joyful or sorrowful, has the potential to teach us valuable lessons and deepen our understanding of ourselves and the world around us.

As we reflect on Chen's story, may we be inspired to cultivate a sense of resilience and acceptance in the face of life's challenges, and to find peace and contentment in the midst of uncertainty and change. For in embracing the wisdom of the lost horse, we discover the freedom to ride the waves of life with grace and courage, knowing that true happiness lies not in the attainment of our desires, but in the acceptance of what is.

The Healing Waters

Restoration and purity flowing from forgiveness and compassion.

In the heart of a dense forest, where sunlight filtered through the canopy of ancient trees and birdsong filled the air with melodies of the wild, there lay a hidden oasis known as the Healing Waters. Legends whispered of its existence, telling tales of miraculous cures and profound transformations wrought by its mystical currents.

Among those who sought the solace of the Healing Waters was a traveler named Kael. Haunted by the shadows of his past, Kael carried within him wounds that ran deep, scars left by betrayals and losses that had left his spirit battered and broken. Desperate for relief from the pain that gnawed at his soul, he embarked on a journey to find the elusive oasis and discover if its healing powers were more than mere myth.

For days, Kael trekked through dense forests and treacherous terrain, his determination driving him forward despite the obstacles that lay in his path. With each step, he felt the weight of his burdens grow heavier, the memories of past hurts weighing heavily on his heart.

But as he drew nearer to his destination, a sense of hope began to blossom within him, fueled by the belief that perhaps, just perhaps, the Healing Waters held the key to his salvation. With each passing day, his pace quickened, his heart racing with anticipation at the thought of finally finding relief from the pain that had haunted him for so long.

At long last, after what seemed like an eternity of wandering, Kael stumbled upon the hidden oasis, its tranquil waters shimmering in the dappled sunlight like liquid gold. With trembling hands, he dipped his fingers into the cool, clear pool, feeling its soothing embrace wash over him like a gentle caress.

As he submerged himself fully in the Healing Waters, Kael felt a wave of warmth and lightness wash over him, his body tingling with the energy of renewal and rebirth. In that moment of surrender, he released the burdens he had carried for so long, allowing them to drift away on the currents of the stream like leaves carried by the wind.

In the embrace of the Healing Waters, Kael found not only physical healing, but a profound sense of peace and acceptance that he had thought forever out of reach. With each passing moment, he felt the wounds of his past begin to heal, replaced by a newfound sense of strength and resilience that he had never known before.

Emerging from the waters, Kael felt reborn, his spirit lighter and his heart full of gratitude for the gift of renewal that the Healing Waters had bestowed upon him. As he journeyed forth into the world once more, he carried with him the wisdom of his experience, knowing that true healing could only be found within the depths of his own heart.

And though the path ahead would undoubtedly be filled with challenges and obstacles, Kael walked it with a newfound sense of purpose and determination, secure in the knowledge that no matter what trials lay ahead, he would always carry with him the healing power of the waters that had set him free.

Reflection:

The story of "The Healing Waters" invites us to reflect on the transformative power of forgiveness and the liberation it brings from past wounds. Through Kael's journey, we are reminded that healing is not just about physical ailments but also about the emotional and spiritual wounds that weigh us down.

The Healing Waters symbolize a sacred space where one can release the burdens of the past and find renewal and rebirth. Kael's experience of submerging himself in these waters mirrors the process of letting go of resentments, grudges, and pain that we carry within ourselves. It reminds us that forgiveness is not about condoning the actions of others but about freeing ourselves from the shackles of anger and bitterness.

Moreover, Kael's transformation serves as a reminder that healing is a deeply personal journey that requires courage, vulnerability, and self-reflection. It is a process of confronting our pain, acknowledging it, and ultimately choosing to release it, even when it feels daunting or impossible.

The story encourages us to consider our own capacity for forgiveness and the ways in which we might be holding onto past hurts. It prompts us to reflect on the healing power of compassion, both for ourselves and for others, and the profound sense of peace that comes from letting go of resentment and embracing forgiveness.

Ultimately, "The Healing Waters" reminds us that while wounds may run deep, they do not have to define us. Through the act of forgiveness, we can find liberation from the past and open ourselves up to a future filled with hope, love, and possibility.

The Kind Baker

The warmth of generosity transforming lives beyond mere sustenance.

In the heart of Millfield, nestled between cobblestone streets and quaint cottages, stood Liam's bakery, a beacon of warmth and hospitality. Its windows displayed an array of freshly baked bread, their golden crusts glistening under the soft glow of the morning sun. The aroma of cinnamon and sugar wafted through the air, inviting passersby to step inside and experience the comforting embrace of Liam's bakery.

Liam himself was a tall, stout man with a twinkle in his eye and a smile that could brighten even the dreariest of days. He had inherited the bakery from his father, and like generations before him, he approached his craft with a sense of reverence and dedication. But it was Liam's kindness that truly set him apart.

One chilly winter morning, as frost clung to the windowpanes and the streets lay silent under a blanket of snow, a weary traveler named Anna stumbled upon Liam's bakery. Her clothes were threadbare, and her face bore the marks of hardship and fatigue. She hesitated at the door, her stomach growling with hunger, unsure if she could afford to buy anything.

Sensing Anna's plight, Liam greeted her with a warm smile and a gentle voice. "Welcome, dear traveler," he said, ushering her inside. "On a cold day like this, a bit of warmth is just what you need."

With that,. Anna's eyes widened in surprise and gratitude as she accepted the gift, her hands trembling with emotion. She had not expected such kindness from a stranger, and it touched her deeply.

"Thank you," Anna whispered, her voice choked with emotion. "Thank you so much."

Liam simply nodded, his smile never faltering. "It's my pleasure, dear traveler. Eat up, and may it bring you comfort on your journey."

As Anna savored the first delicious bite of the bread, warmth flooded her body, driving away the chill of the winter morning. She felt a sense of hope stir within her, a glimmer of light in the darkness of her despair. And in that moment, she knew that she would never forget Liam's kindness.

Determined to repay his generosity, Anna vowed to spread kindness wherever she went. As she continued her journey, she encountered others in need—a homeless man shivering in the cold, a child crying for food—and she shared what little she had with them, just as Liam had done for her.

Meanwhile, back in Millfield, Liam's act of kindness had not gone unnoticed. Word of his generosity spread quickly through the town, and soon, people from all walks of life were flocking to his bakery, eager to experience the warmth and hospitality that had become synonymous with his name.

Moved by Liam's example, his customers began to show more compassion and generosity towards one another. They donated food to the local shelter, helped their neighbors in times of need, and spread kindness wherever they went. And as they did so, they found that the more kindness they gave, the more they received in return.

Years passed, and Liam's bakery became more than just a place to buy bread and pastries—it became a symbol of hope and goodwill in the community. People traveled from far and wide to experience the warmth and generosity that radiated from Liam and his bakery, and they left feeling uplifted and inspired by his example.

Reflection:

"The Kind Baker" serves as a reminder of the transformative power of kindness and compassion in our lives. Liam embodies the essence of generosity and selflessness, demonstrating how even a simple act of kindness can have a profound impact on those around us.

Through Liam's example, we are reminded of the importance of extending a helping hand to those in need, regardless of their circumstances. His willingness to share his bread with Anna not only provided her with nourishment but also offered her hope and comfort in a time of despair. This act of kindness sets off a chain reaction of goodwill, inspiring Anna to pay it forward and spread kindness to others she encounters on her journey.

The story also highlights the interconnectedness of humanity and the ripple effect of our actions. Liam's kindness not only brightens Anna's day but also influences the entire community, as people are inspired to follow his example and show compassion to those around them. This interconnectedness reminds us that even the smallest acts of kindness have the power to create a ripple effect that can touch the lives of countless individuals.

Moreover, "The Kind Baker" underscores the idea that true wealth lies not in material possessions but in the richness of our relationships and the impact we have on others. Despite running a humble bakery, Liam's legacy extends far beyond his storefront, as he becomes known not for his bread alone but for the kindness and generosity that he embodies.

In our own lives, "The Kind Baker" encourages us to cultivate a spirit of generosity and compassion, recognizing that our actions, no matter how small, can make a meaningful difference in the lives of others. It prompts us to look for opportunities to extend kindness to those around us, knowing that even the simplest gestures can bring light and warmth to someone's day. Ultimately, the story invites us to consider how we can contribute to creating a kinder, more compassionate world—one act of kindness at a time.

The Wise Crab

Navigating challenges with strategy and insight overcomes brute force.

In a quaint coastal village nestled between rugged cliffs and the endless expanse of the ocean, there lived a group of fishermen who made their living from the bounty of the sea. Among them was a young fisherman named Kai, known throughout the village for his quick wit and cunning mind.

Kai's days were spent casting his net into the shimmering waters, his weathered hands guiding the worn rope with practiced skill. Each day brought with it the promise of a new adventure, as he braved the unpredictable currents and ever-changing tides in search of the day's catch.

One morning, as Kai set out before dawn, a sense of anticipation filled the air, mingling with the salty tang of the sea. The sky blazed with hues of pink and gold as the sun peeked over the horizon, casting a warm glow upon the sleepy village below.

As Kai cast his net into the water, he felt a sudden tug on the line that sent his heart racing with excitement. With a deft flick of his wrist, he reeled in his catch, only to discover a magnificent crab ensnared in the mesh. But this was no ordinary crab; its shell shimmered like polished silver, and its eyes gleamed with an otherworldly wisdom.

Intrigued by the creature's beauty and intelligence, Kai decided to take it home with him, intending to sell it at the market for a handsome sum. But as he made his way back to the village, a mischievous thought crossed his mind.

"What if I were to keep this magnificent crab for myself?" Kai mused, his eyes lighting up with greed. "Surely, no one would be the wiser."

And so, Kai concealed the crab within his cloak, planning to hide it away until he could find a suitable buyer. But as he approached the village, he heard a voice emanating from beneath his garments—a voice that seemed to echo with the wisdom of the ages.

"Why do you seek to deceive others, young fisherman?" the crab asked, its tone tinged with sadness. "Do you not understand the consequences of your actions?"

Startled by the crab's sudden speech, Kai froze in his tracks, his mind awash with guilt and shame. For in that moment, he realized the error of his ways and the harm he had caused by succumbing to greed and deceit.

With a heavy heart, Kai released the crab back into the sea, vowing to mend his ways and live a life of honesty and integrity. And as he watched the creature disappear beneath the waves, he felt a sense of peace wash over him, knowing that he had chosen the path of righteousness over the allure of wealth and power.

From that day forth, Kai became known as the wisest fisherman in the village, respected not only for his skill on the water but also for the integrity of his character. And though he never forgot the lesson he learned from the wise crab, he carried its teachings with him always, guiding him on the journey of life with humility and grace.

Reflection:

"The Wise Crab" serves as a powerful reminder of the consequences of deceit and the importance of honesty in our interactions with others. Through Kai's journey, we witness the transformative power of self-awareness and the willingness to confront our own shortcomings.

The story invites us to reflect on the choices we make in our own lives and the impact they have on those around us. It reminds us that honesty is not just a virtue but a moral imperative, essential for building trust and fostering meaningful connections with others.

In today's fast-paced world, where the temptation to cut corners and prioritize personal gain often looms large, "The Wise Crab" offers us a timeless lesson in integrity and the importance of staying true to our principles, even in the face of adversity. It challenges us to embrace honesty as a guiding principle in our lives and to cultivate a spirit of integrity that uplifts not only ourselves but all those with whom we interact.

The Four Guardians

Unity and strength found in the diversity of protection.

In the ancient kingdom of Chandrapur, nestled amidst lush forests and towering mountains, there resided four guardians tasked with protecting the realm from harm. Each guardian embodied a different virtue—courage, compassion, wisdom, and integrity—and together, they stood as beacons of hope and guardians of the people.

The first guardian, Aarav, was a towering figure whose presence instilled courage in the hearts of all who beheld him. With muscles honed by years of training and a spirit as fierce as the fire that danced upon his blade, Aarav stood as the epitome of valor and bravery. Countless times, he had charged fearlessly into battle, his unwavering resolve inspiring hope in the face of adversity.

The second guardian, Lila, possessed a heart as vast as the kingdom itself, overflowing with boundless compassion and empathy. Her gentle touch had the power to heal both body and soul, and her words of solace brought comfort to those who found themselves lost in the depths of despair. Whether tending to the sick and injured or offering a listening ear to those in need, Lila's presence brought warmth and light to even the darkest of times.

Arjun, the third guardian, was a sage beyond his years, his mind as sharp as the keenest blade. With a library of knowledge spanning the annals of history and a gift for foresight that bordered on the mystical, Arjun guided the kingdom with wisdom and insight. His counsel was sought by kings and commoners alike, his words of guidance leading the realm through times of peace and prosperity as well as moments of uncertainty and turmoil.

And finally, Maya, the fourth guardian, was a beacon of integrity and righteousness, her unwavering commitment to justice serving as a pillar of strength for the kingdom. With eyes as sharp as an eagle's and a heart as pure as the mountain streams that flowed through Chandrapur, Maya upheld the laws of the land with impartiality and fairness. No injustice could escape her watchful gaze, and no wrongdoer could evade her pursuit of truth and righteousness.

Together, these four guardians formed an unbreakable bond, united in their shared purpose to safeguard the kingdom and uphold the values that defined their character. And though they faced many trials and tribulations along the way, their collective strength and unwavering resolve carried them through even the darkest of times.

But as the years passed and the kingdom prospered under their watchful gaze, the guardians began to grow weary, their spirits weighed down by the burden of their duties. Sensing their plight, the wise sage of Chandrapur came forth with a solution—a quest to find the fabled Fountain of Eternal Youth, said to grant immortality to those who drank from its waters.

And so, the four guardians set out on their journey, traversing treacherous terrain and facing formidable challenges along the way. But despite the obstacles that stood in their path, they remained steadfast in their determination, knowing that the fate of the kingdom depended on their success.

After many trials and tribulations, the guardians finally reached the fabled fountain, its waters shimmering in the light of the setting sun. With hearts full of hope and anticipation, they each took turns drinking from its enchanted waters, their bodies rejuvenated and their spirits renewed.

But as they gazed upon their reflection in the sparkling pool, they realized that their true strength lay not in immortality, but in the virtues that had guided them on their journey—courage, compassion, wisdom, and integrity. And with this newfound wisdom, they returned to Chandrapur, ready to continue their sacred duty of protecting the kingdom for generations to come.

From that day forth, the story of the four guardians became legend in Chandrapur, a testament to the power of virtue and the enduring strength of the human spirit. And though they may have been mortal beings, their legacy lived on in the hearts of all who cherished the values they represented.

Reflection:

"The Four Guardians" not only portrays the timeless virtues of courage, compassion, wisdom, and integrity but also emphasizes the unwavering belief in these virtues as a source of strength and resilience. Aarav, Lila, Arjun, and Maya faced numerous trials and tribulations throughout their journey, but their steadfast faith in the power of their virtues allowed them to persevere even in the darkest of times.

In moments of doubt and uncertainty, it was their belief in the righteousness of their actions that fueled their determination to press forward.

Ultimately, "The Four Guardians" teaches us that it is not enough to simply possess virtues; we must also have unwavering faith in their ability to guide us through life's trials and tribulations. It is this belief that empowers us to overcome obstacles, inspire change, and create a better world for ourselves and future generations.

The Laughing Buddha

Joy and enlightenment in embracing the world as it is.

In the heart of a bustling marketplace, where merchants bartered and shoppers haggled, there lived a humble tea merchant named Liang. Despite the daily hustle and bustle around him, Liang found solace in the simple pleasures of life, content with his modest existence and the joy it brought him.

One day, as Liang sat outside his shop sipping tea, he noticed a traveler passing through the marketplace. The traveler, adorned in tattered robes and with a jovial smile upon his face, carried himself with an air of tranquility and contentment that caught Liang's attention.

Intrigued by the traveler's demeanor, Liang approached him and asked, "Excuse me, sir, but what is the secret to your happiness? You seem to carry a lightness of being that I have never seen before."

The traveler chuckled warmly and replied, "Ah, my friend, the secret to my happiness is simple: I have learned to laugh at life's misfortunes and find joy in every moment, no matter how small or insignificant."

Intrigued by the traveler's words, Liang invited him to share his story over a cup of tea. And so, as they sat together beneath the shade of a blossoming cherry tree, the traveler began to recount his tale.

"I was once a wealthy merchant, with riches beyond measure and possessions aplenty," the traveler began. "But despite all my wealth and abundance, I found myself consumed by greed and dissatisfaction, always yearning for more and never feeling truly fulfilled."

"One day, as I journeyed through the countryside in search of rare treasures, I came across a temple hidden amidst the mountains. Intrigued by its serene beauty, I decided to pay it a visit and seek the wisdom of its resident monks."

"Upon entering the temple, I was greeted by the sight of a laughing Buddha statue, its jovial expression filling the room with warmth and light. Intrigued by its presence, I asked the head monk about the significance of the statue."

"The monk smiled and explained that the laughing Buddha represented the virtues of joy, contentment, and spiritual fulfillment. He told me that true happiness could not be found in material wealth or worldly possessions, but in the acceptance of life's imperfections and the appreciation of its simple pleasures."

"Moved by his words, I decided to renounce my life of luxury and embark on a journey of self-discovery and enlightenment. And though I may not have riches or possessions to call my own, I have found a wealth of joy and contentment in the laughter of the laughing Buddha."

As the traveler finished his tale, Liang felt a sense of peace wash over him, his heart filled with gratitude for the wisdom he had gained. And as they bid farewell to one another and went their separate ways, Liang vowed to carry the traveler's message of joy and contentment with him always, finding fulfillment in the laughter of life's simple pleasures.

Reflection:

The story of "The Laughing Buddha" offers a reflection on the nature of happiness and fulfillment. Through the traveler's journey from wealth to contentment, we are reminded that true joy cannot be found in material possessions or external circumstances alone. Instead, it stems from an inner state of mind, cultivated through acceptance, gratitude, and a willingness to find joy in life's simple pleasures.

The laughing Buddha statue serves as a powerful symbol of this wisdom, embodying the virtues of joy and spiritual fulfillment. Its presence in the temple acts as a guiding light for the traveler, leading him to discover the true source of happiness within himself.

As we reflect on this tale, we are encouraged to examine our own attitudes towards happiness and fulfillment. Are we seeking contentment in external achievements and possessions, or are we cultivating a sense of inner peace and joy that transcends material wealth? By embracing the laughter of life's simple pleasures and finding gratitude in each moment, we can unlock the door to lasting happiness and fulfillment, just like the laughing Buddha.

The Courageous Mouse

Small acts of bravery can lead to monumental changes.

In the heart of a sprawling city, where the towering skyscrapers cast long shadows over the crowded streets below, there lived a young rat named Remy. Born into a bustling colony nestled beneath the bustling metropolis, Remy spent his days scurrying through the labyrinthine alleyways and hidden passages, searching for scraps of food to sustain himself and his family.

But despite the familiarity of his surroundings, Remy felt a restlessness stirring within him—a yearning to explore the world beyond the confines of his underground home. And so, one moonlit night, as the city slept and the stars twinkled overhead, Remy made a bold decision to embark on a journey unlike any he had ever known.

With a sense of excitement and trepidation coursing through his veins, Remy bid farewell to his family and set out into the unknown, his small form illuminated by the soft glow of the moon above. Guided by the light of the stars and the whispers of the night, he ventured forth into the vast expanse of the city, his heart filled with a sense of wonder and possibility.

As he traversed the bustling streets and towering buildings, Remy encountered wonders beyond his wildest imagination. He marveled at the dazzling lights that illuminated the cityscape, the cacophony of sounds that filled the air, and the endless array of sights and smells that assailed his senses at every turn.

But amidst the splendor of the city, Remy also encountered hardship and adversity. He faced dangers lurking in the shadows—hungry predators prowling the streets, treacherous traps laid by human hands, and the constant threat of being swept away by the relentless tide of urban life.

Yet, despite the obstacles that lay in his path, Remy pressed onward, his determination unwavering as he pursued his quest for adventure and discovery. Along the way, he encountered fellow travelers—other rats like himself, each with their own hopes, dreams, and stories to share.

Together, they braved the perils of the cityscape, forging bonds of friendship and camaraderie as they journeyed onward. They traversed bustling thoroughfares and quiet alleyways, dodging traffic and eluding capture as they navigated the maze of urban life.

And as Remy ventured deeper into the heart of the city, he discovered a truth that transcended the boundaries of species and circumstance—a truth that lay not in the destination, but in the journey itself. For in the midst of chaos and confusion, Remy found moments of unexpected beauty and joy—a stolen glance at the shimmering waters of a moonlit river, the soft rustle of leaves in a hidden park, the laughter of children playing in the streets.

And in those moments, Remy realized that the true essence of his journey lay not in the distance traveled or the sights seen, but in the connections forged and the memories made along the way. For in the end, it was the shared experiences and the bonds of friendship that made the journey worthwhile—a journey that would forever live on in the heart and soul of a young rat named Remy.

Reflection:

The tale of "The Rat's Journey" offers a poignant reflection on the universal themes of courage, resilience, and the pursuit of adventure. Through the eyes of Remy, the young rat, we witness the transformative power of curiosity and determination as he embarks on a daring quest to explore the vast unknown of the city.

At its core, the story invites us to consider the inherent human (and rat) desire for exploration and discovery. Remy's journey symbolizes the innate urge to venture beyond the familiar confines of our surroundings, to seek out new experiences, and to embrace the unknown with open arms. In doing so, we may encounter both wonders and challenges, but it is through these encounters that we grow, learn, and ultimately find fulfillment.

Moreover, Remy's journey underscores the importance of perseverance in the face of adversity. Despite the myriad obstacles that he encounters along the way—ranging from hungry predators to treacherous traps—Remy remains steadfast in his resolve to continue forward. Also, the camaraderie that Remy shares with his fellow travelers highlights the significance of human connection and companionship in our lives. As Remy forges bonds with others on his journey, he discovers the profound joy and comfort that comes from shared experiences and mutual support.

Ultimately, "The Rat's Journey" encourages us to embrace the spirit of adventure, to face our fears with courage, and to cherish the connections that sustain us along the way. In doing so, we may find that the greatest treasures lie not at the end of the road, but in the moments of wonder, growth, and friendship that we encounter along the journey of life.

The Melody of Silence

Discovering profound truths in the spaces between sounds.

In the heart of a forest veiled in the gentle embrace of mist resided a wise sage known only as the Silent Sage. His dwelling was a humble abode nestled amidst the ancient trees, where the whispers of the wind and the rustle of leaves served as his constant companions. With each passing day, the Silent Sage immersed himself in the symphony of nature, attuned to its rhythms and harmonies, and found solace in the profound serenity that enveloped him.

Legend had it that the Silent Sage had spent a lifetime in pursuit of inner peace and enlightenment, forsaking the trappings of the material world in favor of a life of simplicity and contemplation. His teachings were whispered among the leaves, carried on the breeze like fragments of a forgotten melody, and those who sought wisdom would often journey to his secluded sanctuary in search of guidance.

One autumn morning, a weary traveler stumbled upon the forest, his footsteps heavy with the weight of his burdens. He had heard tales of the Silent Sage, a sage whose wisdom transcended the boundaries of the mortal realm, and he sought refuge in the sage's tranquil sanctuary, hoping to find answers to the questions that weighed heavily upon his soul.

As the traveler ventured deeper into the forest, guided by the ethereal glow that emanated from the heart of the woods, he felt a sense of peace wash over him, as if the very air around him was infused with a calming energy. At last, he reached a small clearing bathed in dappled sunlight, where the Silent Sage awaited him in silent meditation.

With reverence and awe, the traveler approached the sage, his heart heavy with the burdens of the world. "O wise sage," he whispered, his voice barely more than a breath, "I come to you seeking refuge from the turmoil of life. Please, teach me the secret of your serenity, that I may find peace amidst the chaos."

The Silent Sage regarded the traveler with eyes that seemed to hold the wisdom of the ages. "Listen closely, my child," he said, his voice a soft murmur, "for the melody of silence is all around us, if only we take the time to listen."

With that, the sage closed his eyes and began to hum a soft, wordless melody, a song that seemed to resonate with the very essence of existence. As the traveler listened, he felt a sense of calm wash over him, as if the burdens of the world were lifted from his shoulders, and he was transported to a place of pure tranquility.

In that moment of perfect stillness, the traveler realized that the true secret of the melody of silence lay not in the absence of sound, but in the ability to quiet the mind and open the heart to the beauty of the present moment. For in the silence, he found the peace and serenity that had eluded him for so long, and he knew that he would carry the memory of that sacred melody with him always, a reminder of the infinite potential that lies within each of us.

As the traveler departed from the forest, his heart light and his spirit renewed, he vowed to cherish the wisdom of the Silent Sage and carry it with him on his journey through life. And though the melody of silence may fade from his ears, its echo would forever resonate within his soul, guiding him along the path to inner peace and spiritual fulfillment.

Reflection:

In the tale of "The Melody of Silence," we're reminded of the profound tranquility that can be found in stillness and the quiet moments of introspection. The Silent Sage, living harmoniously in nature, embodies the peace that comes from a deep connection to the world around us.

The story invites reflection on the value of inner serenity amidst life's chaos. Just as the traveler sought solace in the Silent Sage's presence, we, too, can find respite from our struggles by tuning into the subtle melodies of silence within ourselves.

Moreover, the tale underscores the importance of mindfulness and presence. Through the simple act of listening to the song of silence, the traveler discovers a profound sense of calm and clarity, highlighting the transformative power of quiet contemplation.

Ultimately, "The Melody of Silence" encourages us to cultivate moments of stillness in our own lives, allowing us to reconnect with our inner selves and find peace amid life's tumultuous symphony.

The Eternal Flame

The undying light of wisdom that guides through generations.

In the heart of a tranquil temple nestled amidst towering mountains, there flickered an eternal flame—a beacon of wisdom, compassion, and enlightenment that had burned for countless generations. Its origins traced back to the time of the Buddha himself, who, in his quest for truth and enlightenment, had kindled the flame as a symbol of the eternal nature of his teachings.

The temple, known far and wide as a sanctuary for seekers of truth and solace, attracted pilgrims from distant lands who journeyed to bask in the glow of the sacred flame and seek guidance from the wise monks who tended to it. For centuries, the flame had stood as a silent witness to the ebb and flow of human existence, its gentle flicker a reminder of the impermanence of life and the enduring light of the human spirit.

Legend had it that the flame possessed magical properties, bestowing wisdom and enlightenment upon those who approached it with an open heart and a humble spirit. Many stories were told of travelers who had come to the temple burdened by the weight of the world, only to leave with their souls uplifted and their spirits transformed by the power of the eternal flame.

One such traveler, a young woman named Mei Lin, had journeyed from a distant village in search of answers to the questions that had troubled her soul. For years, Mei Lin had felt adrift in the world, her heart heavy with sorrow and her mind clouded by doubt. Despite her best efforts to find peace and contentment, she could not shake the feeling that something was missing from her life—that there was a deeper meaning to existence than she could comprehend.

Guided by an inner voice that whispered of hidden truths and unspoken mysteries, Mei Lin embarked on a pilgrimage to the temple of the eternal flame, her footsteps guided by faith and hope. As she climbed the winding path that led to the temple's sacred halls, her heart swelled with anticipation, the weight of her burdens lifting with each step she took.

At last, Mei Lin reached the temple grounds, where the eternal flame burned bright in the center of a tranquil courtyard, its golden light casting a warm glow upon the faces of those who gathered around it. With trembling hands and a heart full of longing, Mei Lin approached the flame, her eyes shining with tears of gratitude and awe.

As she knelt before the flickering fire, Mei Lin felt a sense of peace wash over her, her fears and anxieties melting away in the warmth of its glow. In that moment of stillness, she felt a connection to something greater than herself—a connection that transcended the boundaries of time and space and united her with the eternal flame and all who had come before her.

For hours, Mei Lin sat in silent meditation, her mind quieted by the gentle rhythm of her breath and the soothing crackle of the fire. In the flickering light of the eternal flame, she glimpsed the secrets of the universe—the interconnectedness of all things, the beauty of impermanence, and the boundless potential that lay within each and every soul.

As dawn broke over the horizon, Mei Lin rose from her meditation, her heart lighter and her spirit buoyed by the wisdom she had gained. With a sense of purpose and clarity that she had never known before, she left the temple behind, knowing that she carried the light of the eternal flame within her, guiding her on the path to self-discovery and enlightenment.

And though her journey was far from over, Mei Lin took comfort in the knowledge that the eternal flame would always be there to illuminate her way, casting its golden light upon her darkest moments and leading her ever onward toward the truth.

Reflection:

The tale of "The Eternal Flame" evokes a profound sense of awe and reverence for the enduring wisdom and guidance that can be found in the teachings of Buddhism. The eternal flame symbolizes the timeless nature of the Buddha's teachings, which continue to illuminate the path for seekers of truth and enlightenment across generations. Its magical properties represent the transformative potential inherent in spiritual practice, offering solace and enlightenment to those who approach it with an open heart and a humble spirit.

Mei Lin's journey to the temple of the eternal flame mirrors the quest for self-discovery and enlightenment that lies at the heart of the Buddhist path. Her struggles with doubt and longing are universal themes, inviting us to reflect on our own spiritual journey and the search for meaning in life.

Through Mei Lin's experience, we are reminded of the importance of mindfulness, meditation, and contemplation in finding inner peace and clarity amidst life's uncertainties. Her encounter with the eternal flame serves as a catalyst for personal growth and transformation, empowering her to embrace the present moment and cultivate a deeper understanding of herself and the world around her.

Ultimately, "The Eternal Flame" inspires us to cultivate the light of wisdom and compassion within ourselves, knowing that it is always there to guide us on our journey towards greater understanding, acceptance, and fulfillment.

The Lost Compass

Finding one's true path requires more than direction - it needs intuition.

In a remote corner of the world, where the towering mountains kissed the sky and the lush forests whispered ancient secrets, existed a village nestled amidst the tranquility of nature's embrace. In this idyllic haven, where time seemed to stand still and the rhythms of life flowed like the gentle currents of a meandering river, lived a humble monk named Chen.

Chen was not just an ordinary monk; he was revered by the villagers for his profound wisdom, compassionate heart, and unwavering commitment to the teachings of the Buddha. Every day, he would rise with the sun, his heart filled with gratitude for the gift of another day, and set out on his journey through the forest, seeking to spread the light of enlightenment to all who crossed his path.

One fateful day, as Chen wandered through the dense undergrowth of the forest, his keen eyes spotted a figure moving amidst the shadows. Drawing closer, he discovered a weary traveler named Liang, who had lost his way in the labyrinthine depths of the woods. Liang's face was etched with worry, his eyes clouded with fear and uncertainty, as he struggled to find his bearings in the dense wilderness.

Moved by Liang's plight, Chen approached him with a gentle smile, his voice soft and soothing like the rustle of leaves in the breeze. "Fear not, my friend," he said, his words carrying the weight of ancient wisdom. "For though the path may seem dark and uncertain, there is always light to guide us on our journey."

With Chen's reassuring presence by his side, Liang felt a glimmer of hope ignite within his heart, dispelling the shadows of doubt that had clouded his mind. As they walked together through the forest, Chen shared with Liang the timeless teachings of the Buddha—lessons of compassion, wisdom, and the interconnectedness of all beings.

As the hours passed and the sun dipped below the horizon, Chen and Liang found themselves deeper in the heart of the wilderness, their footsteps echoing through the silent woods. Yet, despite their efforts, the path ahead remained shrouded in darkness, and Liang's spirits began to falter once more.

But just when all seemed lost, Chen's keen eyes caught sight of a faint glow emanating from the depths of the forest. Following the ethereal light, they stumbled upon a small clearing, where a golden compass lay nestled amidst a bed of wildflowers, its surface shimmering with otherworldly brilliance.

With trembling hands, Liang reached out and picked up the compass, feeling its weight and warmth in his palm. In that moment, he felt a sense of clarity wash over him, as if the answers to all his questions lay within the glowing depths of the compass.

Realizing the significance of this divine gift, Chen gently guided Liang in aligning the compass with the north star, its steady glow illuminating the path that would lead him back to the safety of the village. With a heart filled with gratitude and newfound purpose,

Liang bid farewell to Chen, vowing to honor the teachings he had received and to live his life in service to others.

As Liang disappeared into the darkness, Chen watched him go with a sense of quiet pride, knowing that he had helped another soul find its way home. And as he turned to resume his own journey through the forest, he carried with him the knowledge that true guidance comes not from external sources, but from the light of wisdom that shines within each of us.

Reflection:

In this tale, the encounter of Cheng and Liang symbolizes the transformative power of compassion and guidance. Chen's character serves as a beacon of light, offering solace and wisdom to Liang as he navigates the uncertainties of life. His teachings reflect the timeless principles of Buddhism, emphasizing the interconnectedness of all beings and the importance of cultivating compassion and wisdom.

Liang's journey symbolizes the universal human experience of grappling with fear, doubt, and uncertainty. His encounter with Chen and the discovery of the golden compass represent moments of revelation and enlightenment, where he finds guidance and clarity amidst the darkness of his struggles.

The golden compass itself serves as a metaphor for inner guidance and spiritual insight. Its discovery in the forest signifies the inherent wisdom and guidance available to all who seek it, while its glow represents the illumination of truth and understanding.

Ultimately, the tale underscores the profound impact of compassion, wisdom, and guidance in navigating life's journey. Through Chen's selfless acts and Liang's transformative experience, we are reminded of the power of kindness, knowledge, and inner wisdom to illuminate the path forward and lead us toward greater fulfillment and purpose.

The Magic Bowl

Abundance and gratitude from what seems empty and minimal.

In the heart of a bustling marketplace, where merchants bartered and children played, there lived a humble potter named Wei. Wei was known throughout the village for his skillful craftsmanship and generous spirit. Despite his modest means, he possessed a magic bowl that held a mysterious power.

This. Legend had it that the bowl had the ability to multiply whatever was placed inside it. Some whispered that it was a gift from the heavens, while others believed it was simply the product of Wei's exceptional skill as a potter.

Regardless of its origins, the magic bowl had become a symbol of hope and abundance in the village. People from far and wide would come to Wei's humble pottery shop, hoping to witness the marvel of the multiplying bowl for themselves.

One day, as Wei was preparing to close up shop for the evening, a weary traveler stumbled upon his doorstep. The traveler, his clothes tattered and his eyes filled with longing, begged Wei for a morsel of food to ease his hunger.

Without hesitation, Wei welcomed the traveler into his home and offered him a simple meal of rice and vegetables. As they sat together at the table, Wei noticed the traveler's eyes widen in amazement as he beheld the magic bowl sitting in the center.

Intrigued by the bowl's legendary reputation, the traveler asked Wei if he could see it in action. Without a word, Wei filled the bowl with a handful of rice and placed it in the center of the table. To the traveler's astonishment, the rice began to multiply before his very eyes, until the bowl overflowed with an abundance of food.

Overwhelmed with gratitude, the traveler thanked Wei for his kindness and generosity. But instead of keeping the multiplied rice for himself, Wei insisted that they share it with the other villagers who were in need.

Together, they journeyed through the village, distributing the multiplied rice to those who hungered. With each act of giving, they witnessed the joy and gratitude of the recipients, their hearts filled with a sense of fulfillment and purpose.

As they returned to Wei's home, the traveler marveled at the magic of the bowl and the generosity of its owner. But Wei simply smiled and explained that the true magic lay not in the bowl itself, but in the act of giving without attachment.

For Wei understood that true abundance came not from hoarding wealth or possessions, but from sharing what one had with others. And in that simple act of generosity, he had discovered the greatest treasure of all—the joy of giving from the heart.

The story of the magic bowl spread far and wide, inspiring countless others to embrace the spirit of generosity and compassion. And though Wei's bowl was indeed a marvel to behold, its true power lay in the hearts of those who were touched by its magic.

For in a world filled with scarcity and want, Wei's simple act of kindness served as a beacon of hope and light, reminding all who encountered it that true abundance could be found not in material wealth, but in the richness of the human spirit.

As the years passed, Wei's legend only grew, his name spoken in hushed tones of reverence and awe. But to those who knew him best, he remained the same humble potter, his heart overflowing with love and compassion for all beings.

The magic bowl eventually found its way into the hands of another generation, and its legacy lived on in the hearts of all who had been touched by its power. For as long as there were those who believed in the power of generosity and the magic of the human spirit, the bowl's legend would continue to inspire and uplift all who heard its tale.

Reflection:

The tale of "The Magic Bowl" encapsulates the essence of generosity and selflessness, highlighting the transformative power of giving without attachment. At its core, the story emphasizes the idea that true abundance is not solely measured by material wealth but is found in the act of sharing with others.

Through Wei's example, the story conveys the profound impact that acts of generosity can have on both the giver and the recipient. Wei's willingness to share the multiplied rice not only nourishes the bodies of those in need but also nourishes their spirits, fostering a sense of connection and gratitude within the community.

Furthermore, the tale underscores the idea that true abundance arises from a mindset of abundance, rather than scarcity. Wei's actions demonstrate that when one approaches life with an open heart and a spirit of generosity, opportunities for giving and receiving abound, creating a cycle of abundance that enriches the lives of all involved.

Ultimately, "The Magic Bowl" serves as a reminder of the inherent goodness and generosity that resides within each individual. It encourages us to cultivate a spirit of generosity in their own lives, recognizing that acts of kindness, no matter how small, have the power to create positive change and foster a sense of unity and compassion within society.

The Bodhisattva and the Hungry Tigress

Self-sacrifice as the ultimate act of compassion.

In the heart of a dense forest, where ancient trees whispered secrets to the wind and streams murmured softly as they wound their way through the underbrush, there lived a compassionate Bodhisattva named Ananda. With eyes that sparkled with wisdom and a heart that overflowed with kindness, Ananda wandered the forest paths, offering solace and guidance to all who crossed his path.

One day, as Ananda made his way through the forest, he came upon a scene that filled his heart with sorrow—a hungry tigress lying weak and emaciated beneath the shade of a gnarled oak tree. Her golden fur was matted and dirty, her ribs protruding sharply against her skin, and her eyes glowed with a desperate hunger that pierced Ananda's heart like a dagger.

Moved by compassion, Ananda approached the tigress with caution, his heart brimming with empathy for her plight. With gentle words and soothing gestures, he offered her what little food he had, knowing that it would not be enough to satisfy her hunger but hoping to ease her suffering, if only for a moment.

To his surprise, the tigress accepted Ananda's offering with gratitude, her fierce demeanor softening as she devoured the meager meal. Sensing her deep hunger, Ananda resolved to find more food for her, scouring the forest for berries, roots, and any scraps of food he could find.

As the sun dipped below the horizon and darkness descended upon the forest, Ananda returned to the tigress with his arms laden with food. With tears in his eyes, he watched as she ate, knowing that his small act of kindness had brought relief to her starving belly.

Days turned into weeks, and weeks into months, as Ananda continued to care for the tigress, bringing her food and water and offering her companionship in her time of need. And as he tended to her, he found himself transformed by the experience, his heart expanding with a love and compassion that transcended the boundaries of species and form.

Despite the danger posed by the hungry tigress, Ananda never wavered in his commitment to her welfare, knowing that true compassion knows no bounds. He ventured deeper into the forest in search of food, braving the dangers of the wilderness to ensure that the tigress had enough to eat.

One day, as Ananda sat beside the tigress, watching as she slept peacefully in the dappled sunlight, he realized the true meaning of compassion—that it was not merely an act of kindness, but a recognition of the interconnectedness of all beings, and a willingness to alleviate the suffering of others, regardless of their form or circumstances.

And in that moment, as he gazed upon the sleeping tigress, Ananda understood that true compassion knows no bounds—that it is the light that shines in the darkness, the warmth that melts the coldest heart, and the force that binds us all together in a web of love and understanding.

As the days turned into months and the months turned into years, the tigress grew strong and healthy once more, her golden fur shining in the sunlight and her eyes glowing with gratitude. And though she eventually returned to the wild, her bond with Ananda remained unbreakable, a testament to the transformative power of compassion and the enduring connection between all beings.

Reflection:

"The Bodhisattva and the Hungry Tigress" offers a profound meditation on the nature of compassion and the interconnectedness of all beings. Through Ananda's selfless acts of kindness towards the hungry tigress, we are reminded of the transformative power of compassion to heal wounds, bridge divides, and awaken the innate goodness within us all.

In caring for the tigress, Ananda demonstrates the boundless nature of compassion—that it extends not only to those who look like us or share our experiences, but to all beings, regardless of their species or circumstances. His willingness to alleviate the suffering of the tigress, even at great personal risk, serves as a powerful example for us all, inspiring us to cultivate compassion in our own lives and extend a helping hand to those in need.

As we reflect on Ananda's story, may we be inspired to embody the spirit of the Bodhisattva in our own lives, seeking out opportunities to alleviate the suffering of others and cultivate a sense of connection and compassion that transcends the boundaries of self and other. For in embracing the true meaning of compassion, we discover the path to greater peace, joy, and fulfillment, both for ourselves and for all beings.

The Sacred Grove

The sanctity of nature as a reflection of inner peace.

Deep in the heart of a verdant forest, hidden from the clamor of the outside world, lay a sacred grove known only to a select few. Here, amidst towering trees and lush foliage, the air hummed with a sense of tranquility and reverence, as if the very earth itself exhaled a sigh of contentment.

In this sacred grove, there lived a solitary monk named Kai, who had devoted his life to the pursuit of spiritual enlightenment. Day after day, Kai would retreat to the grove, seeking solace and communion with the divine within the sanctuary of his own heart.

As Kai wandered through the forest, his footsteps falling softly upon the moss-covered ground, he felt a profound sense of connection to the natural world around him. The whispering leaves, the gentle rustling of the wind, and the melodious songs of the birds seemed to speak to him in a language older than words, a language of the soul.

One day, as Kai sat in meditation beneath the shade of an ancient oak tree, he experienced a vision unlike any he had ever known. In his mind's eye, he saw the grove bathed in a soft, golden light, as if touched by the hand of the divine itself.

In the center of the grove stood a magnificent tree, its branches reaching toward the heavens like outstretched arms. Beneath its boughs, Kai saw a shimmering pool of crystal-clear water, reflecting the canopy of stars above with startling clarity.

Drawn by an irresistible pull, Kai approached the pool and gazed into its depths, where he saw his own reflection staring back at him. But instead of seeing himself as he was, Kai saw the radiant light of the divine shining from within, illuminating every fiber of his being with a sense of boundless love and compassion.

In that moment, Kai realized that the sacred grove was not merely a physical place but a state of being—a sanctuary of the heart where the divine spark within each of us could be kindled and nurtured. Here, amidst the beauty and serenity of the natural world, one could find the true source of wisdom and guidance, if only one had the courage to look within.

From that day forward, Kai devoted himself even more fervently to his spiritual practice, spending hours in silent meditation beneath the trees and communing with the divine presence that dwelled within him. And as he delved deeper into the mysteries of the sacred grove, he discovered a wellspring of inner peace and serenity that sustained him through even the darkest of times.

Word of Kai's wisdom and enlightenment spread far and wide, drawing seekers from all corners of the land to visit the sacred grove and learn from the humble monk who called it home. And though Kai welcomed each visitor with open arms and a warm heart, he knew that the true sanctuary they sought could only be found within themselves.

For in the stillness of the heart and the depths of the soul, there lies a sacred grove where the divine spark of the universe resides, waiting patiently to be discovered by those who dare to seek it. And as Kai had learned, it is in this sacred space that we find our true connection to the divine and the source of all creation.

Reflection:

The tale of "The Sacred Grove" resonates deeply with the soul, inviting us to explore the sanctuary of our own hearts and the divine presence that resides within. Through the character of Kai, we are reminded of the transformative power of nature and the profound wisdom that can be found in the stillness of the mind.

The imagery of the sacred grove, with its towering trees and tranquil waters, evokes a sense of peace and reverence that transcends the physical realm. It serves as a metaphor for the inner landscape of our consciousness, where we can retreat from the noise and distractions of the world to connect with our true essence.

Kai's vision of the divine light shining from within mirrors the timeless spiritual truth that we are all manifestations of the same universal consciousness. It reminds us that beneath the surface of our individual identities lies a deeper, unifying essence that binds us all together.

As Kai delves deeper into his spiritual practice, we are invited to reflect on our own journey of self-discovery and inner exploration. Like Kai, we may encounter moments of revelation and insight that illuminate the path ahead and reveal the true nature of our existence.

The tale also emphasizes the importance of compassion and humility in our interactions with others. Despite his profound wisdom, Kai remains humble and open-hearted, welcoming seekers from all walks of life to learn from his teachings. His example reminds us that true wisdom is not measured by knowledge alone but by the depth of our compassion and the sincerity of our intentions.

Ultimately, "The Sacred Grove" encourages us to cultivate a deeper connection to ourselves and the world around us, recognizing the inherent divinity that resides within each of us. It reminds us that even in the midst of life's challenges and uncertainties, we can find solace and guidance in the sanctuary of our own hearts, where the light of the divine shines eternally.

The Golden Thread

The interconnectedness of all lives woven through time.

In the sprawling kingdom of Bhuvaneshwar, nestled amidst the lush greenery of the forest, there lived two souls whose destinies were intricately woven together by the golden thread of fate. Arjun, the young prince of the land, resided in the grandeur of the royal palace, surrounded by opulence and luxury. Despite his privileged upbringing, Arjun felt a sense of restlessness stirring within him, a longing for something beyond the confines of his gilded cage.

Meanwhile, on the outskirts of the kingdom, Maya, a humble weaver, lived a simple yet contented life in her quaint cottage. Her days were spent laboring over her loom, spinning tales of wonder and enchantment into the fabric of her tapestries. Though her abode lacked the grandeur of the palace, Maya possessed a wisdom and serenity that drew others to her like moths to a flame.

One fateful day, as Arjun roamed the forest in search of adventure, he stumbled upon Maya's cottage, nestled amidst a grove of ancient trees. Intrigued by the peaceful aura that surrounded the humble dwelling, Arjun ventured inside, where he found Maya diligently working on her latest creation. The two exchanged greetings, and as they spoke, they felt an undeniable connection stirring between them, as if the threads of their lives were intertwining in a dance of fate.

Over time, Arjun and Maya's friendship blossomed into a deep bond, forged by shared experiences and mutual understanding. Despite their differences in upbringing and status, they found solace in each other's company, drawn together by the invisible threads of destiny that bound them.

As they journeyed together through the trials and tribulations of life, Arjun and Maya encountered challenges that tested their resolve and strengthened their bond. Together, they learned the importance of courage in the face of adversity, the power of compassion in times of strife, and the wisdom of humility in moments of triumph.

Through it all, they remained guided by the golden thread of destiny, which led them on a path of self-discovery and spiritual awakening. They came to understand that their connection was not merely a coincidence but a divine orchestration, a testament to the intricate tapestry of life that binds all beings together.

At its core, the golden thread was more than just a metaphor—it was a tangible expression of the intricate connections that bound every soul to the tapestry of existence. Like the threads of a loom weaving together to create a masterpiece, the golden thread intertwined the lives of all living beings, guiding them on a journey of self-discovery and spiritual awakening.

In the end, Arjun and Maya realized that the golden thread of destiny was not just a guiding force but a source of infinite wisdom and inspiration. They embraced the interconnectedness of all beings and honored the sacredness of life, knowing that they were forever bound together by the threads of fate.

And as they gazed upon the vast expanse of the forest, with its ancient trees and winding rivers, Arjun and Maya felt a deep sense of gratitude and reverence for the golden thread that had brought them together. They knew that their journey was far from over, but they faced the future with courage and conviction, knowing that they walked hand in hand, guided by the unseen hand of destiny.

Reflection:

The tale of the golden thread of destiny is a poignant reminder of the interconnectedness of all beings and the mysterious forces that guide our lives. Through the story of Arjun and Maya, we witness how the invisible threads of fate weave their way through the fabric of existence, drawing together souls from different worlds and guiding them on a journey of self-discovery and spiritual awakening.

At its essence, the golden thread symbolizes the universal web of interdependence that connects every soul to the greater tapestry of life. It is a reminder that we are not isolated individuals but integral parts of a larger whole, each playing a unique role in the unfolding of the universe.

As we reflect on the tale of the golden thread, we are reminded of the beauty and complexity of life's journey. We see how every twist and turn, every triumph and setback, is part of a larger cosmic dance orchestrated by the unseen hand of destiny.

Ultimately, the story of the golden thread invites us to embrace the interconnectedness of all beings and to honor the sacredness of life. It reminds us that we are not alone in this world, but part of a vast and intricate tapestry of existence, woven together by the threads of fate.

The Wise Gardener

Cultivating growth through patience and persistent care.

In a remote village nestled amidst rolling hills and verdant fields, there lived a humble gardener named Ananda. Despite his modest means, Ananda was renowned throughout the land for his wisdom and compassion. His garden, a riot of colorful blooms and lush greenery, was said to be a reflection of his enlightened spirit.

One day, as Ananda tended to his garden with care, a weary traveler passing through the village paused to admire the beauty of his handiwork.

"Your garden is truly magnificent," the traveler exclaimed. "Tell me, what is your secret?"

Ananda smiled kindly, his eyes twinkling with a serene light. "Ah, my friend," he replied, "the secret lies not in the soil or the seeds, but in the heart of the gardener."

Intrigued by Ananda's words, the traveler pressed him for further wisdom. "But how does one cultivate such a garden of tranquility?" he asked.

Ananda gestured toward a bed of vibrant flowers swaying gently in the breeze. "Each bloom in my garden," he explained, "represents a virtue of the heart: kindness, compassion, patience, and forgiveness. By nurturing these qualities within myself, I create a sanctuary of peace and beauty."

The traveler marveled at Ananda's insight, realizing that true abundance could not be measured in material wealth but in the richness of the soul.

Inspired by Ananda's words, the traveler resolved to embark on his own journey of self-discovery. But before he departed, he asked Ananda one final question.

"Tell me, wise gardener," he said, "how do you maintain your garden in the face of adversity and hardship?"

Ananda's smile deepened, his gaze serene yet resolute. "My friend," he replied, "even the most beautiful garden is subject to the changing seasons and the whims of nature. But just as the lotus rises above the muddy waters to bloom in pristine purity, so too can we cultivate inner peace amidst life's challenges."

With a newfound sense of purpose, the traveler bid farewell to Ananda and set out on his journey, carrying with him the gardener's timeless wisdom.

Years passed, and the traveler's wanderings took him to distant lands and far-off shores. Along the way, he encountered trials and tribulations, joys and sorrows, but through it all, he held fast to the lessons he had learned from Ananda.

And when at last he returned to the village of the wise gardener, he found Ananda's garden more beautiful than ever, a testament to the enduring power of the human spirit to transcend adversity and flourish in the light of love and compassion.

As the traveler gazed upon the garden in awe, Ananda appeared at his side, his eyes sparkling with joy.

"Welcome back, my friend," he said. "I see you have discovered the true secret of the garden: that it is not merely a place of beauty, but a reflection of the human soul, nurtured with care and cultivated with love."

Reflection:

The story of the wise gardener offers a profound reflection on the nature of inner peace, resilience, and personal growth.

At its core, the tale illustrates that true abundance and tranquility stem not from external circumstances or material possessions, but from the virtues cultivated within the heart. Ananda, the humble gardener, serves as a symbol of this timeless wisdom, demonstrating that through nurturing qualities such as kindness, compassion, patience, and forgiveness, one can create a sanctuary of peace and beauty amidst life's challenges.

Moreover, Ananda's garden serves as a metaphor for the human soul, susceptible to the changing seasons and uncertainties of life. Yet, through steadfast resolve and inner strength, individuals can weather adversity and emerge stronger and more resilient, like the lotus rising above the muddy waters to bloom in pristine purity.

The traveler's journey of self-discovery and growth mirrors the universal quest for meaning and fulfillment. His encounters with Ananda and the lessons learned along the way underscore the transformative power of reflection and introspection. By delving into the depths of his own heart and embracing the wisdom imparted by the wise gardener, the traveler discovers that true abundance lies not in the pursuit of external accolades or achievements, but in the cultivation of inner peace and authenticity.

Ultimately, the story invites us to reflect on our own lives and the gardens of our hearts. It prompts us to consider the virtues we wish to nurture within ourselves and the resilience we aspire to cultivate in the face of life's inevitable trials. Through reflection on the timeless wisdom of the wise gardener, we are reminded of the profound truth that true happiness and fulfillment emanate from within, rooted in the richness of the human spirit.

The Moonlit Path

Illumination and clarity arriving in quiet, reflective moments.

In a remote village nestled at the foot of towering mountains, there lived a young monk named Surya. From an early age, Surya had felt a deep calling to the path of enlightenment, drawn by the promise of inner peace and spiritual awakening.

One moonlit night, as Surya sat in silent meditation beneath the ancient Bodhi tree, he heard a gentle rustling of leaves and felt a soft breeze caress his skin. Opening his eyes, he beheld a figure standing before him: a wise old monk with eyes that gleamed like polished jewels.

"Greetings, young one," the old monk said, his voice a melodious whisper. "I have come to offer you guidance on your journey."

Surya bowed respectfully, his heart fluttering with anticipation. "Please, master," he said, "teach me the path to enlightenment."

The old monk smiled knowingly, his gaze piercing the depths of Surya's soul. "The path to enlightenment is like a moonlit path," he began. "It is shrouded in darkness, yet illuminated by the radiant light of wisdom and compassion."

With that, the old monk gestured toward the distant mountains, where the moon cast its silvery glow upon the earth below. "Follow me," he said, leading Surya down a winding trail that meandered through the dense forest.

As they walked, the old monk spoke of the trials and tribulations that lay ahead: the temptations of desire, the illusions of ego, and the shadows of fear that threatened to obscure the path. But he also spoke of the virtues that would guide Surya on his journey: patience, perseverance, and unwavering faith in the power of love.

At last, they emerged from the forest onto a moonlit clearing, where a tranquil pond shimmered in the pale light. Reflecting the heavens above, its surface was a mirror of stars, each one a glimpse of the infinite cosmos.

"Here," the old monk said, "is where your journey truly begins."

With a gentle smile, he motioned for Surya to kneel beside the pond and gaze into its depths. As Surya peered into the still waters, he saw his own reflection staring back at him: a young monk with eyes alight with curiosity and longing.

"Look closely, my son," the old monk whispered. "What do you see?"

Surya studied his reflection intently, searching for answers amidst the ripples of moonlight. And then, with sudden clarity, he understood.

"I see myself," he said, "but I also see the universe. I see the interconnectedness of all things, the ebb and flow of life itself."

The old monk nodded, his eyes shining with pride. "Indeed," he said. "In every reflection lies the potential for enlightenment. Embrace the light within you, and let it guide you on your journey."

With those words, the old monk vanished into the night, leaving Surya alone with his thoughts and the gentle rustling of leaves. And as he gazed up at the moon, its luminous glow filling him with a sense of peace and purpose, Surya knew that he had found his true path: the moonlit path of enlightenment.

Reflection:

"The Moonlit Path" offers a poignant reflection on the journey of spiritual awakening and the pursuit of enlightenment. Through the experiences of the young monk Surya, the story delves into themes of guidance, self-discovery, and the transformative power of inner wisdom.

The moonlit night serves as a symbolic backdrop for Surya's journey, representing the interplay between light and darkness, clarity and uncertainty. As Surya encounters the wise old monk, he is drawn into a deeper understanding of the path ahead, one that is both illuminated by wisdom and veiled in mystery.

The guidance offered by the old monk echoes the timeless teachings of Buddhism, emphasizing the importance of virtues such as patience, perseverance, and compassion. These virtues are portrayed as essential companions on the journey toward enlightenment, helping Surya navigate the challenges and temptations that lie ahead.

The tranquil pond becomes a metaphor for self-reflection and introspection, inviting Surya to confront his own inner doubts and fears. Through the act of gazing into its depths, Surya gains insight into the interconnectedness of all things and the boundless potential within himself.

Ultimately, "The Moonlit Path" encourages us to contemplate their own journey of self-discovery and spiritual growth. It reminds us that enlightenment is not a destination to be reached, but a path to be embraced—one that requires courage, humility, and a willingness to face the unknown.

The Weaver's Daughter

Weaving fate with the threads of diligence and faith.

In a quaint village nestled amidst rolling hills and shimmering streams, there lived a skilled weaver named Amara. With nimble fingers and a creative spirit, Amara wove intricate tapestries that captured the beauty of the natural world and the essence of human emotion.

But despite her talent, Amara harbored a deep sense of longing within her heart. She yearned to unravel the mysteries of existence, to discover the true purpose of her life beyond the loom and the threads.

One day, as Amara sat at her loom, lost in thought, a gentle breeze stirred the air, carrying with it the faint strains of a melodious song. Intrigued, Amara followed the sound to the edge of the village, where she discovered a group of monks gathered beneath a towering Bodhi tree.

Entranced by the peaceful aura that surrounded the monks, Amara approached them with a humble bow. "Forgive me, revered monks," she said, "but I could not help but be drawn to your presence. Might you share with me the wisdom of your teachings?"

The eldest monk, a sage with eyes that sparkled like polished stones, regarded Amara with a knowing smile. "Of course, my child," he said. "But first, tell us of your own journey. What is it that brings you to us?"

And so, Amara recounted her tale to the monks, speaking of her longing for purpose and her desire to unravel the mysteries of life. Moved by her sincerity, the monks welcomed Amara into their fold, inviting her to join them on their journey of spiritual discovery.

Under the guidance of the monks, Amara embarked on a journey of self-discovery and enlightenment. Together, they delved into the teachings of the Buddha, exploring the nature of suffering, the impermanence of existence, and the path to liberation.

As the days turned into weeks and the weeks turned into months, Amara found solace and inspiration in the company of her newfound companions. With each passing day, her understanding deepened, and her heart grew lighter with the knowledge that she was on the path to true fulfillment.

But amidst the serenity of the monastery, a shadow loomed on the horizon. News reached the village of an impending invasion by a neighboring kingdom, threatening to engulf the land in chaos and despair.

Determined to protect her home and her people, Amara made the difficult decision to leave the monastery and return to the village. With a heavy heart, she bid farewell to her companions, knowing that the path ahead would be fraught with danger and uncertainty.

Upon her return to the village, Amara rallied her fellow villagers to prepare for the impending invasion. With courage and determination, they fortified their defenses and stood united in the face of adversity.

When the enemy finally arrived, they were met not with swords and spears, but with a spirit of compassion and resilience. Inspired by Amara's leadership and the teachings of the Buddha, the villagers chose to embrace their enemies as brothers and sisters, rather than adversaries.

And in the end, it was not through force of arms, but through the power of compassion and understanding, that peace was restored to the land. The village, once threatened by destruction, flourished once more, united in a bond of harmony and compassion that transcended all boundaries.

And though Amara's journey had taken her far from the loom and the threads of her craft, she knew that her true purpose had been found—not in the intricacies of her tapestries, but in the threads of compassion and understanding that wove together the fabric of her life.

Reflection:

"The Weaver's Daughter" offers a profound reflection on the themes of purpose, self-discovery, and the transformative power of compassion.

At its core, the tale invites readers to contemplate the universal quest for meaning and fulfillment. Through the character of Amara, who feels a deep sense of longing despite her skill as a weaver, the story speaks to the inherent human desire to uncover the mysteries of existence and find one's true purpose in life.

Amara's journey of self-discovery begins when she encounters a group of monks and is drawn to the wisdom of their teachings. This reflects the idea that true enlightenment often arises from a willingness to explore new paths and embrace unfamiliar perspectives. It also highlights the importance of seeking guidance and inspiration from others on the journey toward self-awareness and fulfillment.

As Amara delves into the teachings of the Buddha and immerses herself in the company of the monks, she undergoes a profound transformation. Her understanding deepens, and she discovers a sense of peace and purpose that had eluded her before. This underscores the transformative power of spiritual practice and the pursuit of knowledge in shaping one's identity and worldview.

However, Amara's journey takes an unexpected turn when her village faces the threat of invasion. In choosing to leave the monastery and return to her community, she demonstrates a commitment to service and a willingness to confront adversity in order to protect those she loves. This reflects the idea that true fulfillment is often found not in personal enlightenment alone, but in the service of others and the pursuit of a greater good.

Ultimately, it is through acts of compassion and understanding that peace is restored to the land. Amara's leadership and the villagers' choice to embrace their enemies as brothers and sisters highlight the transformative power of empathy and reconciliation in overcoming conflict and division.

In reflecting on "The Weaver's Daughter," we are invited to consider our own journey of self-discovery and the role of compassion in shaping our relationships and interactions with others. The story serves as a reminder that true fulfillment is found not in the pursuit of individual success or material wealth, but in the cultivation of empathy, understanding, and a sense of purpose that transcends the boundaries of the self.

The Simile of the Saw

Endurance and equanimity amidst life's severest tests.

In the ancient city of Shravasti, nestled amidst the tranquil plains of Northern India, the Buddha resided in the Jetavana Monastery, surrounded by his devoted disciples. One day, a group of monks approached the Enlightened One seeking guidance on how to respond to criticism and harsh words.

Sensing their earnestness, the Buddha began to impart his wisdom through the Simile of the Saw, a teaching that would illuminate the path to inner peace and equanimity.

"Monks," the Buddha began, his voice calm and gentle, "when others criticize you with harsh words, you should train yourselves thus: 'Our minds will remain unaffected, and we shall utter no harsh words in return. We shall abide compassionate for their welfare, with a mind of loving-kindness, without inner hatred.'"

To illustrate his point, the Buddha shared a parable of two woodcutters. One day, as they toiled in the forest, they engaged in a heated argument over the division of labor. The first woodcutter, feeling aggrieved by the words of his companion, lashed out with harsh words in retaliation.

The second woodcutter, however, remained calm and composed, refusing to be drawn into conflict. Instead, he responded with gentle words and a peaceful demeanor, diffusing the tension between them.

Observing this, the first woodcutter was puzzled and asked his companion, "Friend, you have been insulted, abused, and attacked, yet you remain peaceful. Why is that?"

The second woodcutter replied, "If someone gives you a gift, but you choose not to accept it, to whom does the gift belong?"

The first woodcutter pondered this question for a moment before realizing the profound truth of his companion's words. By refusing to accept the harsh words directed at him, the second woodcutter had deprived them of their power to cause harm.

Turning to the assembled monks, the Buddha explained that just as the second woodcutter had remained unaffected by the harsh words of his companion, they too should cultivate a mind of equanimity in the face of criticism and blame.

He likened praise and blame to a saw that cuts through the mind, causing suffering when one becomes attached to either. By remaining unaffected by both, the mind becomes like an uncut gem, untarnished by the vicissitudes of worldly judgment.

The Buddha's teaching resonated deeply with the monks, who listened attentively to his words, realizing the profound truth of his guidance. From that day forth, they endeavored to cultivate equanimity in the face of praise and blame, responding with kindness and compassion to all beings.

As they continued on their spiritual journey, the monks carried the Simile of the Saw with them as a guiding light, a reminder of the Buddha's timeless wisdom and the path to inner peace and liberation. And in the quietude of the monastery, amidst the rustling of leaves and the gentle murmur of the breeze, they found solace and serenity, knowing that they were walking the path of the Enlightened One.

Reflection:

The Simile of the Saw offers profound insights into the nature of human interaction and the cultivation of inner peace. Reflecting on this Buddhist tale prompts us to contemplate our responses to criticism and harsh words in our own lives.

At its core, the story teaches the importance of maintaining equanimity in the face of adversity. Like the second woodcutter who remained unaffected by his companion's harsh words, we are reminded of the power of inner strength and resilience. Instead of reacting impulsively or defensively, we can choose to respond with calmness and compassion, thereby diffusing conflict and promoting harmony.

Moreover, the simile underscores the transient nature of praise and blame. Just as a saw cuts through wood, the Buddha likens praise and blame to a tool that can cause suffering when we become attached to either. By recognizing the impermanence of external judgments and cultivating a mind of equanimity, we free ourselves from the fluctuations of worldly opinion and find refuge in the unchanging depths of our own inner peace.

In our daily lives, we may encounter situations where criticism or praise threatens to disturb our mental equilibrium. In such moments, the Simile of the Saw serves as a guiding principle, reminding us to anchor ourselves in mindfulness and compassion. Through the practice of non-reactivity and loving-kindness, we can navigate the ups and downs of life with grace and dignity, cultivating a sense of inner peace that remains unshakeable amidst the storms of circumstance.

Ultimately, the reflection on the Simile of the Saw invites us to consider how we can embody the teachings of the Buddha in our interactions with others. By cultivating a mind of equanimity and responding to criticism and praise with kindness and compassion, we not only contribute to our own well-being but also create a ripple effect of positivity and harmony in the world around us.

The Ten Bulls

The stages of enlightenment unfolding in the quest for self-realization.

Once upon a time, in a serene village nestled amidst verdant hills and meandering streams, there lived a young seeker named Koji. From the tender age when he first felt the stirrings of curiosity within his heart, Koji knew that his destiny lay in uncovering the mysteries of existence and understanding the true nature of reality.

Guided by an inner calling, Koji embarked on a journey of self-discovery, setting forth with nothing but a sense of wonder and a longing for truth. As he wandered through the countryside, he encountered wise sages and humble monks, each offering their own pearls of wisdom and guidance along his path.

It was during one such encounter that Koji first heard whispers of a legendary bull—a majestic creature said to roam the land, holding the key to enlightenment within its very being. Intrigued by the tales, Koji resolved to seek out the elusive bull and unlock the secrets of the universe.

And so, with a heart full of hope and a spirit brimming with determination, Koji set out on his quest, following the faint traces and hidden signs that pointed the way. Through dense forests and rugged mountains, across vast deserts and rushing rivers, he journeyed, his eyes ever fixed on the horizon.

After many days of searching, Koji finally came upon a tranquil meadow bathed in the soft glow of dawn, where the bull grazed peacefully amidst the swaying grasses. As he approached the magnificent creature, Koji felt a deep resonance stirring within him—a recognition of his own inherent Buddha nature mirrored in the calm gaze of the bull.

In that moment of profound connection, the veil of illusion was lifted, and Koji saw clearly the truth that had eluded him for so long. He realized that the bull symbolized the essence of his own being—the untamed spirit of awakening that lay dormant within him, waiting to be discovered.

With newfound clarity and purpose, Koji resolved to capture and tame the bull, symbolizing the process of mastering the unruly mind and harnessing its wild energies. Through discipline and practice, he learned to cultivate inner strength and resilience, guiding the bull with gentle firmness along the path of enlightenment.

As Koji rode the bull triumphantly homeward, he felt a sense of joy and gratitude wash over him, knowing that he was journeying toward the ultimate destination of awakening. With each step, he embodied the teachings of the Buddha, integrating wisdom into everyday life and finding solace in the simple joys of existence.

Yet, even as Koji transcended the bull and realized the emptiness of all phenomena, he understood that his journey was far from over. With humility and compassion, he returned to the source, sharing the fruits of his realization with all beings and dedicating himself to the liberation of the world.

And so, Koji returned to the village, his heart filled with peace and contentment, knowing that he had walked the path of the Ten Bulls and emerged transformed. In the hustle and bustle of the market place, he found serenity amidst the chaos, embodying the timeless wisdom of the Buddha in every moment.

Reflection:

The tale of the Ten Bulls offers profound insights into the journey of self-discovery and enlightenment, inviting reflection on our own paths of growth and awakening.

At its core, the story speaks to the universal longing for truth and meaning that resides within each of us. Like the young seeker Koji, we are drawn to explore the depths of our own being, seeking to unlock the secrets of existence and understand our place in the universe.

As we embark on this journey, we encounter challenges and obstacles along the way, symbolized by the various stages of Koji's quest to capture and tame the bull. Each stage represents a different aspect of the path, from the initial seeking and discovery to the eventual realization of our true nature and the transcendence of self.

Through discipline and practice, we learn to master the unruly energies of the mind and cultivate inner strength and resilience. We ride the bull triumphantly homeward, integrating wisdom into everyday life and finding joy and contentment in the present moment.

Yet, even as we reach the pinnacle of realization and transcendence, we understand that the journey is never truly complete. Like Koji, we return to the source, sharing the fruits of our realization with others and dedicating ourselves to the liberation of all beings.

In this way, the tale of the Ten Bulls serves as a powerful reminder of the timeless wisdom of the Buddha and the path to awakening that lies within each of us. It encourages us to reflect on our own journeys of self-discovery and to embrace the challenges and obstacles that arise along the way as opportunities for growth and transformation.

As we navigate the ups and downs of life, may we draw inspiration from the timeless teachings of the Ten Bulls, finding solace and guidance in the eternal quest for truth and enlightenment. And may we walk the path with humility and compassion, knowing that the journey itself is the ultimate destination, and that the truest fulfillment lies in the journey of awakening itself.

The Wandering Cloud

Freedom in detachment, flowing effortlessly with life's currents.

In the vast expanse of the azure sky, there drifted a solitary cloud, wispy and ethereal, its form ever-changing as it journeyed across the boundless heavens. This cloud, known as the Wandering Cloud, was said to possess a wisdom that surpassed the ages—a wisdom born of its ceaseless wanderings and contemplations.

As the Wandering Cloud drifted lazily across the horizon, it observed the world below with keen awareness, its gaze falling upon the bustling cities, the serene mountains, and the tranquil rivers that crisscrossed the landscape. With each passing moment, the cloud absorbed the sights and sounds of the world, reflecting upon the ephemeral nature of existence and the interconnectedness of all things.

In its wanderings, the Wandering Cloud encountered many beings—creatures of the earth and sky, each with their own hopes and fears, joys and sorrows. Yet, amidst the endless tapestry of life, the cloud remained detached and impartial, observing the ever-changing dance of existence with a sense of equanimity and acceptance.

One day, as the Wandering Cloud drifted over a remote mountain monastery nestled amidst mist-shrouded peaks, it caught sight of a group of monks engaged in deep meditation. Intrigued by their serene countenances and tranquil demeanor, the cloud descended gently upon the monastery, enveloping it in a soft embrace.

In the presence of the Wandering Cloud, the monks felt a sense of peace and tranquility wash over them, their minds free from distraction as they entered into a state of deep meditation. With each breath, they felt a profound connection to the cloud above, as if it were whispering ancient truths to them from beyond the veil of the heavens.

For days and nights, the Wandering Cloud lingered above the monastery, casting its benevolent gaze upon the monks as they delved deeper into the mysteries of existence. And in that timeless space between the earth and sky, the boundaries between self and other dissolved, and the monks experienced a sense of oneness with all creation.

As the days turned into weeks and the weeks into months, the Wandering Cloud continued on its journey, drifting ever onward across the vast expanse of the sky. Yet, in the hearts of the monks, its presence lingered like a distant memory—a reminder of the timeless wisdom that resides within each of us, waiting to be discovered.

And so, the Wandering Cloud became a symbol of enlightenment and liberation, a beacon of hope and inspiration for all beings who seek to awaken to the truth of their own existence. For in its ceaseless wanderings, the cloud embodied the boundless potential of the human spirit to transcend the limitations of the physical world and soar to the heights of spiritual realization.

As the sun set behind the distant mountains and the stars began to twinkle in the night sky, the Wandering Cloud disappeared from view, its form dissolving into the vastness of the heavens. And yet, in the hearts of all who had encountered it, its presence remained etched like a silent prayer—a reminder of the timeless wisdom that dwells within us all, waiting to be revealed in the stillness of our own hearts.

Reflection:

The tale of the Wandering Cloud offers a captivating journey into the realms of contemplation and enlightenment, inviting reflection on the nature of existence and the pursuit of inner peace.

At its core, the story illustrates the beauty of detachment and impartial observation embodied by the Wandering Cloud. As the cloud drifts across the sky, it observes the world with a sense of equanimity, unaffected by the joys and sorrows of mortal existence. This detachment serves as a powerful reminder of the importance of cultivating inner peace and tranquility amidst the ever-changing landscape of life.

The encounter between the Wandering Cloud and the monks at the mountain monastery highlights the transformative power of presence and mindfulness. In the presence of the cloud, the monks experience a profound sense of peace and unity, transcending the boundaries of self and other to connect with the timeless wisdom of the universe. This serves as a poignant reminder of the potential for spiritual awakening that lies within each of us, waiting to be discovered through the practice of meditation and contemplation.

Moreover, the Wandering Cloud serves as a symbol of enlightenment and liberation, inspiring all beings to embark on their own journey of self-discovery and realization. Its ethereal presence reminds us of the boundless potential of the human spirit to transcend the limitations of the physical world and soar to the heights of spiritual realization.

As we reflect on the tale of the Wandering Cloud, we are invited to contemplate the nature of our own existence and the path to inner peace and enlightenment. Like the cloud, may we learn to observe the world with equanimity, embracing each moment with mindfulness and acceptance. And may we be inspired to embark on our own journey of self-discovery, knowing that the wisdom we seek lies within the depths of our own hearts, waiting to be revealed in the stillness of our own being.

The Laughing Monk

Finding humor and wisdom amidst life's paradoxes.

In a tranquil monastery nestled amidst emerald forests and mist-covered mountains, there lived a monk whose laughter echoed through the halls like the tinkling of wind chimes on a gentle breeze. This monk, known simply as Brother Kiku, possessed a rare gift—a boundless sense of joy and humor that uplifted the spirits of all who crossed his path.

From the moment he entered the monastery as a young novice, Brother Kiku was known for his infectious laughter and irrepressible cheerfulness. While his fellow monks spent hours in solemn meditation and silent contemplation, Brother Kiku could often be found frolicking in the gardens, playing pranks on his brethren, or bursting into fits of laughter at the slightest provocation.

Despite his playful nature, Brother Kiku was deeply revered by his fellow monks for his unwavering commitment to the path of enlightenment. Beneath his jovial exterior lay a heart of profound compassion and wisdom, honed through years of diligent practice and introspection.

One day, a group of travelers arrived at the monastery seeking guidance on their spiritual journey. Intrigued by tales of the laughing monk, they sought out Brother Kiku in the hopes of receiving his wisdom and insight.

As the travelers approached Brother Kiku's humble abode, they were greeted by the sound of his laughter echoing through the courtyard. Stepping inside, they found the monk sitting cross-legged on a woven mat, his eyes twinkling with mirth as he regaled his companions with tales of his misadventures.

"Welcome, friends!" Brother Kiku exclaimed, his laughter bubbling forth like a mountain spring. "What brings you to our humble monastery on this fine day?"

The travelers bowed respectfully to Brother Kiku and explained their quest for spiritual guidance. They spoke of their struggles and doubts, their fears and aspirations, seeking answers to the timeless questions that had plagued humanity since time immemorial.

Brother Kiku listened intently to their words, his laughter gradually subsiding as he contemplated their plight. With a gentle smile, he spoke words of comfort and wisdom, offering insights that touched the hearts of all who listened.

"Life is but a fleeting moment, filled with both joy and sorrow," Brother Kiku began, his voice soft and melodic. "But it is our laughter that sustains us through the darkest of times, reminding us of the beauty and wonder that surrounds us in every moment."

He shared tales from his own journey—the moments of triumph and adversity, laughter and tears—that had shaped his understanding of the world. Through his stories, the travelers glimpsed the profound truth that lay hidden beneath the surface of their own experiences, finding solace and inspiration in Brother Kiku's words.

As the sun dipped below the horizon and the stars began to twinkle in the night sky, the travelers bid farewell to Brother Kiku, their hearts filled with gratitude and newfound understanding. In his laughter, they had found the key to unlocking the secrets of the universe—the timeless wisdom that lies within each of us, waiting to be discovered in the joy of the present moment.

And as they journeyed onward, guided by the laughter of the monk, they carried with them a sense of peace and contentment, knowing that they had encountered a true master of the art of living—a laughing monk whose laughter would echo through the ages, reminding all who heard it of the boundless joy that lies at the heart of existence.

Reflection:

The tale of the Laughing Monk offers a delightful exploration of the profound wisdom that can be found in joy and laughter. It prompts reflection on the importance of cultivating a lighthearted spirit amidst the challenges of life.

At its essence, the story celebrates the transformative power of laughter as a means of connecting with the present moment and finding solace in the midst of adversity. Brother Kiku, with his infectious laughter and irrepressible cheerfulness, serves as a beacon of light in the monastery, reminding his fellow monks and travelers alike of the beauty and wonder that surround us in every moment.

Through Brother Kiku's laughter, we are reminded that life is a precious gift to be cherished and celebrated, regardless of the circumstances we may face. His ability to find humor and joy in even the most mundane of tasks speaks to the resilience of the human spirit and the boundless potential for happiness that resides within each of us.

As we reflect on the tale of the Laughing Monk, we are invited to contemplate the role of joy and laughter in our own lives. In a world often fraught with uncertainty and turmoil, may we draw inspiration from Brother Kiku's example, cultivating a spirit of lightheartedness and compassion that uplifts not only ourselves but all those around us.

The Lotus Sutra

The blossoming of universal enlightenment from the mud of earthly existence.

In the heart of a verdant grove, where the rustle of leaves and the chirping of birds created a symphony of nature's melodies, there gathered a diverse assembly of seekers eager to receive the teachings of the Buddha. Among them was a humble monk named Kulananda, whose heart overflowed with reverence and devotion as he awaited the arrival of the enlightened one.

As the sun began its slow descent towards the horizon, casting a golden glow upon the tranquil landscape, the Buddha emerged from the depths of the forest, his presence radiating a sense of peace and serenity that enveloped all who beheld him. With a gentle smile upon his lips, he seated himself upon a lotus throne, his disciples gathering around him in rapt attention.

With a voice that echoed like the gentle breeze rustling through the leaves, the Buddha began to expound upon the teachings of the Lotus Sutra, a profound scripture that held the key to unlocking the mysteries of existence and the path to enlightenment. As he spoke, his words carried the weight of wisdom accumulated over countless lifetimes, guiding his listeners on a journey of self-discovery and spiritual awakening.

The Lotus Sutra, the Buddha explained, was a profound exposition on the nature of reality and the boundless potential for enlightenment that resides within each and every being. It taught that all sentient beings possess the Buddha nature—the inherent capacity for wisdom, compassion, and liberation—and that the path to enlightenment lay open to all who sought it with sincerity and dedication.

Through parables and metaphors, the Buddha illuminated the timeless truths contained within the Lotus Sutra, teaching his disciples the importance of cultivating compassion, wisdom, and skillful means in their quest for liberation. He spoke of the Bodhisattva path, the noble journey of selfless service and altruistic intention that leads to the ultimate goal of Buddhahood.

As the teachings unfolded, a sense of awe and wonder filled the hearts of those gathered, their minds expanding to encompass the vastness of the Buddha's wisdom and the boundless compassion that flowed from his heart. Each word uttered by the enlightened one seemed to penetrate to the very core of their being, igniting a spark of realization and insight that illuminated the path before them.

As the sun dipped below the horizon, signaling the end of the day's teachings, the disciples bowed in gratitude to the Buddha, their hearts filled with a sense of deep reverence and awe. For in the Lotus Sutra, they had found not only a roadmap to enlightenment but a source of inspiration and guidance that would accompany them on their journey through samsara's endless cycles.

As they dispersed into the gathering twilight, their minds abuzz with the profound teachings they had received, the disciples carried with them the timeless wisdom of the Lotus Sutra, a beacon of light to illuminate their path and guide them towards the ultimate goal of liberation and awakening. And in the heart of the tranquil grove, the echo of the Buddha's teachings lingered like the sweet fragrance of a lotus blossom, a reminder of the boundless potential that resides within each and every being.

Reflection:

The teachings of the Lotus Sutra illuminate the profound truths of existence, offering a roadmap for those seeking enlightenment and liberation from suffering. Through the Buddha's exposition, we are reminded of the inherent Buddha nature within us all—a spark of divine wisdom and compassion that transcends the limitations of the ego and the illusions of the material world.

The Lotus Sutra teaches us the importance of cultivating qualities such as compassion, wisdom, and skillful means in our spiritual journey. It encourages us to embrace the Bodhisattva path—a path of selfless service and altruistic intention that leads to the ultimate goal of Buddhahood. By embodying the spirit of the Bodhisattva, we can alleviate the suffering of all sentient beings and work towards the realization of our true nature.

As we reflect on the teachings of the Lotus Sutra, we are called to deepen our understanding of the interconnectedness of all things and the profound potential for awakening that lies within each moment. We are reminded that enlightenment is not a distant goal to be attained but a present reality to be realized in the here and now.

May the wisdom of the Lotus Sutra inspire us to cultivate compassion, wisdom, and mindfulness in our daily lives, guiding us towards the ultimate goal of liberation and awakening. And may we walk the path with humility, gratitude, and reverence, knowing that the teachings of the Buddha are a timeless source of guidance and inspiration for all beings.

Conclusion:

As we reach the end of our journey together, we hope that "Stories of Serenity" has served as a source of inspiration and guidance on your path to self-discovery and personal growth. Through the timeless wisdom of Buddhist teachings, may you find the courage to embrace life's challenges with compassion, cultivate inner peace amidst the chaos, and discover the profound joy that comes from living in alignment with your truest self.

In "52 Stories of Serenity," each tale is a thread in the intricate fabric of wisdom that has been woven from the profound teachings of Buddhism. As we traverse from "The Mustard Seed" to "The Two Acrobats," we uncover layers of lessons about resilience, mindfulness, and the art of living with compassion and inner peace.

Reflect on the journey of Maya in "The Mustard Seed," whose quest for comfort amidst sorrow leads her to understand the universal nature of grief, echoing the teachings in "The Arrow Maker," where focus and purpose in crafting each arrow mirror our need to lead intentional lives. This theme of mindfulness is beautifully paralleled in "The Tiger and the Strawberry," where the fleeting sweetness of the strawberry teaches us to savor every moment amidst life's impermanence.

The wisdom of perspective and mutual understanding in "The Blind Men and the Elephant" complements the tale of "The Precious Gem," illustrating how our desires and searches for fulfillment often overlook the riches we already possess. These stories collectively teach us about the limitations of our perceptions and the expansive nature of true understanding, as seen in "The Salt Doll," who dissolves in the ocean to become one with the vastness it sought to comprehend.

In "The Elephant Rope," we learn about the mental chains that restrict us, a motif that is intricately linked to "The Dog's Empty Dream," where aspirations and realities converge to teach us about acceptance and transformation. These tales encourage us to break free from self-imposed limits, a lesson that resonates with "The Jar of Honey," where each taste of honey becomes a metaphor for the sweetness of living fully and consciously.

Consider the relational dynamics explored in "The Four Wives," which delve into the complexities of love and attachment. This narrative complements the story of "The Golden Fish," where the fisherman's wish reveals the ephemeral nature of desire and the profound realization that true contentment comes from within. This understanding is mirrored in "The Lotus Flower," emerging pristine from muddy waters, symbolizing purity and enlightenment beyond material attachments, much like the "Tree of Life" which stands as a testament to our interconnected existence with nature and each other.

"The Two Acrobats" skillfully depict the balance between risk and trust, a balance crucial in navigating the answers provided in "The Three Questions," where the most important time, person, and action converge to teach us about the essence of mindful living. "The Woodcutter's Wealth" brings us back to the richness found in simplicity, celebrating the natural beauty that surrounds us, a theme that dances through "The Peacock's Dance," where beauty and individual expression paint a vivid picture of life's vibrant tapestry.

As we reflect on these tales, let us weave their moral fabrics into the quilt of our daily lives. "52 Stories of Serenity" offers more than narratives; it presents a philosophy, a way to view the world, and a path to walk with awareness, empathy, and tranquility. These stories are beacons that guide us through our own journeys, encouraging us to reflect, understand, and transform.

Carry forward the spirit of these teachings. Let them be your companions in the quiet moments of introspection and your guides in the bustling chaos of life.

Remember, the journey to serenity is ongoing, and each moment offers an opportunity for growth and transformation. As you navigate the ups and downs of life, may these stories serve as beacons of light, guiding you towards a life of greater meaning, purpose, and fulfillment, serene in the knowledge that peace is not found in the world around us, but within us.

Acknowledgments:

We extend our heartfelt gratitude to all those who have contributed to the creation of this book, including the authors, teachers, and practitioners whose wisdom has inspired its pages. We also thank you, dear reader, for joining us on this journey and for embracing the transformative power of storytelling in your quest for serenity.

If you have found joy or solace in these stories, please consider sharing your experience by leaving a review. Your feedback not only supports our work but also helps other seekers on their path to enlightenment and understanding.

Printed in Great Britain
by Amazon